Endorsed By The Business Continuity Institute

Endorsed by The Disaster Recovery Institute International

BUSINESS CONTINUITY PLANNING:
A STEP-BY-STEP GUIDE WITH PLANNING FORMS

THIRD EDITION

Kenneth L. Fulmer, CBCP
Certified Business Continuity Planner

Philip Jan Rothstein, FBCI, Editor

This book includes reproducible worksheets and forms, PLUS sample plans, templates, and more! Download instructions are on the last book page.

The Rothstein Catalog On Disaster Recovery
Rothstein Associates Inc.
Brookfield, Connecticut USA
www.rothstein.com

ISBN 1-931332-21-5

Disclaimer

License Statement

ISBN 1-931332-21-5

Rothstein Associates Inc., Publisher
The Rothstein Catalog On Disaster Recovery
4 Arapaho Rd.
Brookfield, Connecticut 06804-3104 USA
203.740.7444 or 1-888-Rothstein (888.768.4739)
203.740.7401 fax
www.rothstein.com
info@rothstein.com

CONTENTS

DISASTER RECOVERY INSTITUTE INTERNATIONAL

Belinda Wilson
CBCP, Vice Chairperson DRII

In today's business environment, change is the norm. The path to your business goals is seldom marked, and never direct. Success in this world demands agility and resilience, and relies on its ability to easily adapt and be flexible in a world of uncertain times. An adaptive infrastructure that tightens integration and synchronization between IT resources and business processes while delivering a level of interoperability that supports the requirements for a new infrastructure ecosystem. An adaptive infrastructure delivers virtualized resources as services in response to business process requirements. It scales or redeploys resources quickly and efficiently as the business requires, in a single department or across the entire enterprise. To adapt effectively to change in the business environment, the infrastructure itself must deliver services continuously, secure against attack and threat.

But continuous, secure operations are more than a step toward somewhere else: they are a destination of their own. It is time to begin the journey toward an infrastructure that can serve as a dependable foundation for your business today, and the engine of quick, smooth adaptation to business requirements in an unpredictable future.

Businesses build cultures of business continuity by planning, then overcoming everyday threats and obstacles, until continuity is no longer optional but rather is built into the company's corporate culture. Never complete, the process cycles through analysis, building, integration, management and evolution. With every turn, your business becomes more secure, efficient and agile in its response to both challenge and opportunity.

The continuity and security of your business are not isolated destinations. Even your first steps will bring you toward a broader, more integrated operational vision. And efficiencies will only improve as employees move together toward common objectives. As you go, the path will get easier. Protecting and organizing information systems helps you pick up speed-moving ahead with new sophistication and efficiency. Your systems will become not just safer, but easier to use and manage for employees, partners and customers.

No destination is final, but the journey toward continuous operations brings its own practical, measurable rewards along the way. And with every step, your business grows more resilient, more agile and better prepared to take advantage of the next business change.

This book demonstrates the changing focus of business continuity moving it outside of IT and into the boardroom. Decisions surrounding business continuity are no longer involving only the technical provisioning but are business driven to help ensure companies are "always on" and thus competitive. The book supports the processes and guidelines set forth in DRI International's (DRII) approach to ensure a successful implementation of a business continuity program and is a good starting point for someone new to the industry.

ABOUT DRI INTERNATIONAL

Disaster Recovery Institute International (DRII) was first formed in 1988 as the Disaster Recovery Institute in St. Louis, Missouri. A group of professionals from the industry and from Washington University in St. Louis forecast the need for comprehensive education in business continuity. Alliances with academia helped shape early research and curriculum development.

The group also understood that individual certification and establishing a Common Body of Knowledge (standards) could only enhance industry professionalism. As a result, the new nonprofit organization established its goals:

> *to promote a base of common knowledge for the business continuity planning/disaster recovery industry through education, assistance, and publication of the standard resource base; certify qualified individuals in the discipline; and promote the credibility and professionalism of certified individuals.*

DRII sets standards that provide the minimum acceptable level of measurable knowledge, thus providing a baseline for levels of knowledge and capabilities. Accordingly, in 1997, DRII, together with the Business Continuity Institute (BCI, www.thebci.org), published the **Professional Practices for Business Continuity Planners** as the industry's international standard. For more information about DRII, please visit **www.drii.org**.

Belinda Wilson, CBCP
Executive Director, Hewlett-Packard, Business Continuity Services
Vice-Chairperson, DRII
August, 2004

THE BUSINESS CONTINUITY INSTITUTE

Larry Kalmis, FBCI
Chairman, BCI

Kenneth Fulmer, CBCP has produced an important and useful guide for the business continuity planning novice. This clear, concise work will also be a valuable reference for the advanced practitioner.

Mr. Fulmer upholds many of the principles you will find promoted and supported by the Business Continuity Institute and encouraged as part of Business Continuity Management good practices.

In more than thirty years as a business continuity practitioner, I have seen many small and medium-size businesses pay the penalty for lack of preparedness. Often, overwhelmed by the jargon employed by many practitioners and the mistaken concepts that business continuity is too costly, that it is only for the "big boys," and that they do not have the resources or knowledge base, they choose to take the risk instead. For many, it is an unfortunate choice because much can be done with reasonable commitment to avoid business disruptions or mitigate the impact for those that are unavoidable.

In this excellent primer, Mr. Fulmer sets out a simple, concise, and, most of all, logical roadmap both for developing the justification for a business continuity / disaster recovery program as well as for developing and maintaining the resultant plan. He starts by leading you through the assessment of potential risks and impacts establishing the business case, which, after all should be the ultimate driver for any commitment of staff and other resources to business continuity. Mr. Fulmer then, using straightforward, jargon-free, checklists, tables, and worksheets, takes you step-by-step through generally accepted "good practices," enabling you to construct an appropriately sized recovery plan.

This book clearly puts forth the rationale, concepts, and mechanics for business continuity planning in an easy-to-use format for the business continuity initiate. The advanced practitioner will also find this book a practical reference and its checklists, tables, and worksheets a useful toolkit.

Larry Kalmis, FBCI
Project Executive, Virtual Corporation
Chairman, the Business Continuity Institute
October, 2004

About The Business Continuity Institute

The Mission of the **Business Continuity Institute** is to promote the art and science of business continuity management.

The Business Continuity Institute (BCI) was established in 1994 to provide opportunities to obtain guidance and support from fellow professionals. The Institute provides an internationally recognized status in relation to the individuals experience as a continuity practitioner. The BCI has over 1650 members in 45 countries.

The wider role of the BCI is to promote the highest standards of professional competence and commercial ethics in the provision and maintenance of business continuity planning and services.

The Aims and Objectives of the BCI

*   To define the professional competencies expected of business continuity professionals

*   To provide an internationally recognized Certification scheme for the business continuity profession.

*   To provide a program of Continuous Professional Development to enable members to maintain their professional competencies.

*   To initiate, develop, evaluate and communicate BCM thinking, standards and good practices

*   To influence policymakers, opinion-formers and other stakeholders worldwide in Business Continuity Management.

www.thebci.org

Endorsed by The
Business Continuity
Institute

PREFACE
Melvyn Musson
FBCI, CBCP, CISSP

One of the first things that one needs to do when asked to write the preface to a book, is to determine what you feel the book's niche will be. In this case, the book has a very specific niche as a down-to-earth, practical "primer" or introduction to Business Continuity Planning, particularly for small and medium-sized firms.

It will also help answer the questions "what have I got myself into?" and "what is covered by Business Continuity Planning?" These are questions which someone with little or no Business Continuity Planning experience will ask themselves immediately after they are informed that they are now responsible for such planning within their firm, or that they are now charged with developing such a plan for the firm.

Other books can provide more depth of detail that may subsequently be needed, but this book will enable someone with little or no experience to start to put together a project plan, determine what they need to include in the initial structure of the plan and identify those areas that they may need to research further. Someone with more experience will find this book a useful resource to make sure they have covered all the bases. Worksheets, forms and action items are located throughout the book to provide that initial information base on which to build a plan.

This book provides the basic information to enable firms to start the development of their plans in the "classical" business continuity planning manner. Alternatively if one wishes to approach the plan in a different manner, possibly due to corporate culture issues, the book still provides an information base that can assist one in developing your own project and plan documentation.

One other advantage of starting with this book is that the reader starts from a simple beginning and can build to more detail, as that becomes necessary. This point is a key consideration. There is a tendency when developing a Business Continuity Plan to make it more complicated and detailed than may be necessary, particularly in small or medium-sized firms.

The Rt. Hon. David Blunkett, presently the Home Secretary in the United Kingdom Government, said recently in the Foreword to a new booklet "Expecting the Unexpected: Business Continuity in an Uncertain World" that Business Continuity and planning is just as important for small firms as it is for large corporations and that plans need to be simple but effective, comprehensive but tailored to the needs of the organization.

This book will put those, particularly in small and medium-sized firms, on the track to develop simple but comprehensive plans tailored to the needs of their organizations. Although written with an IT bias, one can extrapolate from the IT to determine what needs to be done by the business units or from an overall business perspective.

For those wanting to research Business Continuity Planning further, the Disaster Recovery Institute International (www.drii.org) and the Business Continuity Institute (www.thebci.org) have developed a set of Professional Practices for Business Continuity Planners. These comprise 10 subject areas of a common body of knowledge that characterizes the profession. Each subject area contains a description of the area, the role of the professional and an outline of the knowledge that the professional should demonstrate within that subject area.

Melvin Musson

Fellow, Business Continuity Institute (FBCI)
Business Continuity Planning Manager
Internal Audit
Edward Jones
St. Louis, Missouri, USA
September, 2004

PREFACE
Philip J. Rothstein
FBCI

For some organizations, Business Continuity (BC) Planning is a fact of life — dedicated staff, budget and resources devoted to continually developing, exercising, validating, maintaining and enhancing their ongoing Business Continuity Management programs. For the typical business whether large or small, reality usually gets in the way.

A colleague of mine used to say that Business Continuity had its own specific gravity: It never quite sank to the bottom of the pile of priorities, but never quite rose to the top. It was always next (or next but one) on the list of things that had to be done.

Every business owner or manager knows they need to address business continuity — some day — after putting out day-to-day fires, paying the bills, taking care of customers, and catching their breath. So, what are those of us who have the luck to operate in the real world, supposed to do about business continuity?

The answer is obvious — do what you can realistically accomplish with whatever time and resources you are able to spare. Of course, you should ensure your BC program meets any legal, contractual or regulatory requirements — and meets your fiduciary responsibilities.

In this book and companion CD-ROM, Ken Fulmer has provided us with a clear, easy-to-use resource for business continuity: a step-by-step tool which isn't going to overwhelm you nor break the bank, yet which will provide you with a sound foundation for beginning on the path to effective business continuity. While there are more complex tools and books available, this Guide will get your BC program going surprisingly fast and with a lot less sweat and tears than you might expect. It will also give you a structure which you can continue to build on as your business changes and evolves, and as you are willing and able to devote more resources to business continuity.

My advice to the reader is to do the best you can, as soon as you can, to address the business continuity requirements of your organization — your business' survival may depend on it!

Philip Jan Rothstein
Fellow, Business Continuity Institute (FBCI)
President, Rothstein Associates Inc.
Brookfield, Connecticut USA
October, 2004

PREFACE
Andrew Hiles
FBCI

We had an international prospect in a financial district. He had been talking about implementing a business continuity project for around eighteen months — but there was no real sign of movement on it. We had one final try to persuade him to go ahead with the project, identifying disasters that had happened in the district and to similar organizations. At the meeting, he said "Yes, we ought to get round to it. But it will never happen to us." The following month there was an explosion in the area, damaging his offices. I telephoned him and asked him if he was now convinced of the case for business continuity. "Yes," he said. "We have just authorized spending $15 million on a second site."

We do not all have the luxury of a budget of that size. But there is always something meaningful that we can do to reduce risk, protect our assets and plan for continuity and recovery.

Time is the crucial element. The first few hours following a disaster is the time when recovery success or failure is decided. A plan is vital to put order into chaos and to make the most of those crucial early hours — and the days that follow.

This book provides practical advice, easy to follow formats and checklists that will help its readers to understand, reduce and manage the risks to their organization. It gives step-by-step guidance on how to develop, test and maintain plans to handle emergencies, protect people and ensure business continues — come what may.

Andrew Hiles
Fellow, Business Continuity Institute (FBCI)
President, Kingswell International Limited
Oxford, United Kingdom
August, 2004

INTRODUCTION

Devastating acts like the September 11, 2001 terrorist attacks in New York and Washington, D.C. have left many businesses and individuals concerned about the possibility of future threats and their potential impacts on us. Recent PricewaterhouseCoopers research, www.pwcglobal.com, from public sources has revealed that the financial impacts from these attacks were staggering:

- An estimated 14,600 businesses inside and around the World Trade Center were impacted by the disaster.

- 13.4 million square feet of space in six buildings in and surrounding the WTC complex were destroyed.

- 36 miles of new cable had to be installed by the New York electric utility, Consolidated Edison.

- 652 companies occupying 28.6 million square feet of space were temporarily or permanently displaced by the destruction.

- 200,000 communication lines were knocked out by network failures.

- 12,000 Con Edison customers had their electric power fail.

"In addition to the direct impacts of the attacks on September 11, the indirect impact to U.S. businesses has been estimated at $151 billion in the first year" — *Fortune*, February 18, 2002.

However, there are things you can do to prepare for the unexpected that will give you a measure of control over the effects of a disaster.

Whether it is caused by terrorist activity, nature, technical problems or human error, any emergency can force catastrophic consequences and enormous costs on your business. The result: property damage, interruption of operating procedures, lost profits and even your competitive standing.

In emergencies, it is critical that you make the right decisions and bring the immediate threat to your company and your employees under control quickly. Your company must resume its most important functions in an emergency mode as quickly as possible. At the time of a disaster, the one thing that all companies have working against them is time. Lost time translates into dissatisfied customers, lost revenue, and more.

Many existing Business Continuity Plans today are too complicated and have not been well maintained. The September 11th attacks have caused us to question more than ever, how useful our plans would really prove to be.

Traditionally, disaster recovery planning has focused on computer systems. However, recovering business operations includes more than just the computer system. Thought needs to be given to such issues as long distance service, secure locations where employees can work, and the salvage or replacement of building contents. Because mission-critical functions usually depend on technology and telecommunications networks, rapid recovery of these is very important, but is of little value without also recovering enterprise-wide business operations.

Many organizations have mainframe and minicomputer recovery plans in place. However, it is important for us to recognize that over time, many of our applications may have migrated to distributed decentralized environments with fewer controls and less security.

A plan for business continuity will be worth your effort and can be considered an asset, but only if you follow through on these essential steps:

- Before a disaster strikes, identify all computer systems, applications, people, equipment and supplies needed for recovery.

- Have a back-up procedure for critical files and systems, and a secure off-site storage facility.

- Have one or more alternate places to go for data processing and business operations.

- Be able to maintain effective control over the recovery effort.

- Identify outside resources that can assist you in the recovery process.

- Test your plan to evaluate its capability to provide the required level of support for your core business process and ultimate recovery.

- Maintain the plan. Depending on a plan that is out-of-date can be worse than having no plan at all.

While this book and accompanying CD-ROM provide a comprehensive approach to business continuity and recovery, it is not intended to be a substitute for professional, legal or financial advice. It is designed to help planning coordinators focus on key points to explore while developing Business Continuity Plans for their companies.

WHY SHOULD YOUR BUSINESS

PREPARE FOR A DISASTER?

This chapter contains a description of the types of disasters your company might experience and the potential financial and legal ramifications that could follow.

By the end of this chapter you will:

- Understand the importance of Business Continuity Planning

- Become aware of the potential interruptions that could effect your company's bottom line

- Understand what's at stake if you do not plan

- Understand the potential legal consequences of not planning

This book subscribes to the well known rule, BE PREPARED! By planning ahead for an emergency you can help defend your business against irreparable damage or even total business failure. The time taken to plan for an emergency could be the best investment your company ever made.

WHAT DISASTER MIGHT HIT YOU?

Disasters may occur at any time for many reasons. A Business Continuity Plan (BCP) must be in place to prevent or reduce the effects of disasters. According to The Disaster Recovery Institute International (*www.drii.org*), 93% of companies who experience a disaster without a recovery plan close within five years. Fifty percent of companies that lose critical business functions for more than ten days never recover. For Fortune 500 companies, business and system downtime costs an average of $96,000 per minute!

There are many types of disasters that can affect your company's bottom line. Do you have a Business Continuity Plan to manage your way through these?

Equipment Failure	Fire	Hazardous Material
Windstorms	Civil Disturbance	Incident
Biological/Radiological	Water Pipe Breakage	Extended Power Outage
Incident	Earthquake	Communications Failure
Flooding	Loss of Key Employees,	Explosion
Cyber Crime	Supplier or Customer	Transportation Accidents
Denied Access	Network failure	Terrorist Attack

If your answer is "yes," then take your plan out, dust it off and use this guide to assess and update your plan. If your answer is no, you are not alone and it is time to dig into this book and to begin protecting your company's assets.

IT'S TOO MUCH WORK! WHY SHOULDN'T WE JUST TAKE THE RISK?

Company management too often neglects disaster planning. The most common reasons are: lack of time and resources, lack of top management support, lack of money, too many causes of disasters to plan for effectively, little awareness of potential hazards, and lack of knowledge in developing a plan. We have all heard at least one of these reasons for not having a plan, but are any really good enough to risk the consequences of not being prepared?

Here's a simple test. Can you answer "yes" to all the following questions? If not, how would the repercussions affect your company's ability to remain in business?

1.   Are you confident that you will manage through a disaster better than your competition? If not, how much business are you likely to lose?

2.   Are you ensuring the safety of your personnel and customers? If not, could your legal liability put the company under?

3.   Are you prepared to deal with the media, your stockholders and your employees when a disaster strikes?

4.   Have you taken steps to eliminate or minimize the threat of fire, flooding, employee sabotage, cyber attack, etc.?

5.   Are your company's vital records adequately protected?

The obvious reasons for planning, like avoiding financial ruin, maintaining market share and minimizing negative publicity, are important ones. But there is another convincing reason for Business Continuity Planning: avoiding potential legal problems.

LEGAL REASONS FOR HAVING A PLAN

Protecting the confidentiality, integrity and availability of a patient's medical information is no longer just a best practice for healthcare entities, but a legal requirement.

As passed by the United States Congress, the *Health Insurance Portability and Accountability Act of 1996 (HIPAA) - PL 104-191 Standards for Privacy of Individually Identifiable Health Information - 45 CFR Parts 160 and 164*, institutes administrative reforms that have been phased in over the period from 2000 through 2003. Of major importance in the HIPAA legislation is the issue of data and transaction standardization — a mandate very few healthcare providers can circumvent if they bill third parties for services provided to patients. The HIPAA regulations apply to "covered entities," groups that include health plans, health care clearinghouses, and health care providers that transmit any health information in electronic form. The law also changes the way the "covered entities" have to protect the privacy of a patient's health information, and contains security procedures that must be followed to protect the integrity of a patient's health information. For more information on the Health Insurance Portability and Accountability Act of 1996 go to www.cms.hhs.gov/hipaa.

Other legal reasons for Business Continuity Planning and disaster recovery capability have been categorized to respond to a law, statute or regulation that specifically requires your business to have a disaster recovery plan. Contingency Planning and Research, Inc. categorized these applicable statutes into 5 areas. Each area is presented here, but is not intended by Contingency Planning and Research, Inc. to be all-inclusive:

- **Contingency Planning Statutes** — Apply to the development of plans to ensure the recoverability of critical systems. Example: Federal Financial Institutions Examination Council (FFIEC). The FFIEC guidelines replace previously issued Banking Circulars, BC-177, BC-226, etc.

- **Liability Statues** — Establish levels of liability under the "Prudent Man Laws" for directors and officers of a corporation. Example: Foreign Corrupt Practices Act (FCPA).

- **Life and Safety Statutes** — Set out specific ordinances and standards for ensuring the protection of employees in the workplace. Examples: National Fire Protection Association (NFPA), Occupational Safety & Health Administration (OSHA).

- **Risk Reduction Statues** — Stipulate areas of risk management required to reduce and/or mitigate the effects of a disaster. Example: Office of the Comptroller ("OCC"); Circular 235 and Thrift Bulletin 30.

- **Security Statutes** — Cover areas of computer fraud, abuse and misappropriation of computerized assets. Example: Federal Computer Security Act.

• **Vital Records Management Statutes** — Specifications for the retention and disposition of corporate electronic and hard-copy records. Example: IRS Records Retention requirements.

Statutory Example

The Federal Financial Institutions Examination Council (FFIEC), consisting of the Board of Governors of the Federal Reserve System, the Federal Deposit Insurance Corporation, Office of the Comptroller of the Currency, Office of Thrift Supervision, and the National Credit Union Administration, issued on May 20, 2003 revised guidance for examiners and financial institutions on business continuity planning. The FFIEC also issued guidance to bank examiners on the supervision of technology service providers. The guidance is contained in two booklets.

The *Business Continuity Planning* Booklet provides guidance and examination procedures to assist bank examiners in evaluating financial institution and service provider risk management processes to ensure the availability of critical financial services.

The *Supervision of Technology Service Providers* Booklet covers the supervision and examination of services performed for financial institutions by technology service providers. It outlines the agencies' risk-based supervision approach, the supervisory process, and the examination ratings used for technology service providers.

The guidance stresses that an institution's management and board of directors have the ultimate responsibility for ensuring outsourced activities are conducted in a safe and sound manner and in compliance with applicable laws and regulations.

These booklets represent the latest in a series of updates to the 1996 FFIEC *Information Systems Examination Handbook*. The FFIEC is updating the Handbook to address significant changes in technology since 1996 and to incorporate a risk-based examination approach. The updates are being issued in separate booklets that will ultimately replace all chapters of the Handbook and comprise the new *FFIEC Information Technology Handbook*.

The booklets are being distributed electronically and are available at www.ffiec.gov/guides.htm.

Determining Liability

Other legal reasons are that most businesses have contracts with one another, and some may require that their suppliers perform, no matter what happens. Banks, manufacturers, insurance companies and other businesses are aware of the importance of Business Continuity Planning. These businesses obviously do not want to bite the dust if their suppliers fail to deliver after a disaster. So, review your contracts closely. If you provide services to another company, you may be required by contract to have a continuity plan that has been tested and proved reliable. Even if contracts include a "Force Majeure" clause limiting liability in extreme circumstances, you could still lose business partners, suppliers or clients.

Many attorneys know another reason as "common law." Common law grew out of court decisions and some very old laws. Many of the laws today regarding negligence and fiduciary responsibilities were assembled out of the common law.

In a common law instance, your company may have fiduciary obligations and "duties of care" to its shareholders and customers. Plaintiff attorneys can be extremely creative in drawing up duties of care for businesses, whether they are manufacturers, medical providers, service bureaus or whatever type of business. Many jurisdictions require directors and officers of companies to exercise what is called "good business judgment." This is a legal term that is used a lot in litigation. Good business judgment can also apply to Business Continuity and Recovery Management.

Considering the cost of lawsuits alone, doesn't it make good business sense to have a Business Continuity Plan in place?

In the long run, a reliable plan could save your company big bucks, its very survival and even your job!

Considering what is at stake, what better time than now to get started!

You will find worksheets throughout this book to help you develop your plan easily and effectively. The forms are also included on the "Planning Forms CD-ROM" in Microsoft Word® format. Refer to the PLEASE READ ME FIRST file on the CD-ROM for information about copying the forms to your hard drive.

2

GETTING STARTED

> This chapter discusses the basic considerations required to ensure a successful recovery, the different types of plans, and then introduces you to the beginning activities of the planning process.
>
> By the end of this chapter you will:
>
> - Understand the basic requirements needed to ensure business continuity
>
> - Understand the difference between plan types and ultimately what your plan should accomplish
>
> - Have completed Steps 1 thru 3: Writing the Purpose, Objectives, Scope and Assumptions; Identifying the plan Coordinator and Development Team; Assigning Action Items, Coordination Responsibilities and Timeframes

BASIC CONSIDERATIONS

As you begin to prepare your plan, keep in mind that the goal is to ensure that you have the following basics if a disaster strikes:

1.   An alternate business location;

2.   Access to vital records and resources during the recovery;

3.   Key people assigned to the recovery effort; and,

4.   A plan for a speedy recovery

AN ALTERNATE BUSINESS LOCATION

If an event occurs preventing access to your facility, or if it is totally destroyed, your company must have an alternate location in which it can function, such as a vacant room or facility that could be easily equipped for your needs. If your business is so dependent upon computers that even a few minutes of downtime affect the bottom line, consider a fully equipped and operational location somewhere else.

VITAL RECORDS

Keep all records necessary to restore critical department functions off-site. Although some will not be needed for days or weeks after a disaster, eventually all need to be recovered.

KEY PEOPLE

The recovery process requires the necessary company staff, plus outside vendors and civil agencies.

A PLAN

A reliable and up-to-date plan will decrease your recovery time. Should your facility be destroyed, important information regarding your vendors, recovery teams and disaster notification procedures will be critical. Waiting to make your recovery plan at the time disaster strikes can be disaster itself.

HOW MANY PLANS?

Some companies have just one plan for the entire organization and others have a plan for every computer system, application, or other resource. Other approaches plan for each core business, with separate plans, as needed, for critical resources. Ultimately, your Business Continuity Plan will properly prepare your response, recovery and continuity of business for disruptions affecting the data center, the business functions you support and the company's other critical processes. If you choose to develop more than one plan, there must be coordination during their development and future updates to ensure recovery efforts and supporting resources neither negate each other nor duplicate efforts.

TYPES OF PLANS

In general, universally accepted definitions for disaster recovery and related planning areas have not been available. This has sometimes led to confusion regarding the actual scope and purpose of various types of plans. Therefore, the scope of your plan(s) may vary from the descriptions below.

- **Business Continuity Plan** (BCP) — The BCP focuses on sustaining an organization's business functions during and after a disruption. An example of a business function may be your payroll process or accounts receivable process. A Continuity Plan may be written for a specific business function or may address all key business functions. The data center or Information Technology (IT) is considered in the BCP in terms of its support to the larger business processes, although today, many businesses practice the further reaching process of BCP to ensure that the whole end-to-end business process can continue if a serious incident occurs.

- **Business Recovery Plan** (BRP) — also **Business Resumption Plan**. The BRP addresses the restoration of business processes to ensure that IT Services can recover and continue after an emergency. The BRP is similar to the BCP, but unlike that plan, the BRP typically lacks procedures to ensure continuity of critical processes throughout an emergency or disruption.

- **Continuity of Operations Plan** (COOP) — the COOP focuses on restoring an organization's essential functions at an alternate site and performing those functions for up to 30 days before returning to normal operations. The Federal Emergency Management Agency (FEMA), which is the Government's executive agent for COOP, provided COOP guidelines in *FPC 65*, (www.fas.org/irp/offdocs/pdd/fpc-65.htm), *Federal Executive Branch Continuity of Operations*. Standard elements of a COOP include a Delegation of Authority statement, Orders of Succession, and Vital Records and Databases. Because COOP emphasizes the recovery of a government agency operational capability at an alternate site, the plan does not necessarily include IT operations. In addition, minor disruptions that do not require relocation to an alternate site are typically not addressed. In accordance to PDD-63, *Critical Infrastructure Protection*, COOP plans for systems critical to supporting the nation's infrastructure must be in place by May 2003.

  Government agencies with essential functions at federal, state and local levels have always had continuity plans. The Continuity of Operations (COOP) directives provided by the Office of Management and Budget (OMB) and the President of the United States outline the objectives of Business Continuity Planning for all federal departments and agencies.

- **Disaster Recovery Plan** (DRP) — As suggested by its name, the DRP applies to major, usually catastrophic, events that deny access to your facility for an extended period. Frequently, DRP refers to an IT-focused plan designed to restore operations of a disrupted system, application or computer facility at an alternate location after an emergency.

- **Incident Response Plan** — The Incident Response Plan establishes procedures to address cyber attacks against your company's IT system(s). These procedures are designed to enable your security personnel to identify, mitigate, and recover from malicious computer incidents, such as unauthorized access to the IT systems, denial of service attacks, or unauthorized changes to your system hardware or software such as malicious virus, worm, or Trojan horse attacks.

- **Occupant Emergency Plan** (OEP) — The OEP provides the response procedures for the occupants of your facility in the event of a situation posing a potential threat to the health and safety of personnel, the environment or property. Such events would include fire, hurricane, terrorist attack or a medical emergency. OEPs are usually developed at the facility level, specific to geographic location and structural design of your building.

Plan	Purpose	Scope
Business Continuity Plan (BCP)	Provide procedures for sustaining essential business operations while recovering from a significant disruption.	*Addresses business processes; IT addressed based on its support for business process*
Business Recovery (or Resumption) Plan (BRP)	Provide procedures for recovering business operations immediately following a disaster	*Addresses business processes; not IT focused; IT addressed based only on its support for business process*
Disaster Recovery Plan (DRP)	Provide detailed procedures to facilitate recovery of capabilities at an alternate data site	*Often IT-focused; limited to major disruptions with long-term effects*
Continuity of Operations Plan (COOP)	Establish procedures and capabilities to sustain an organization's essential, strategic functions at an alternate site for up to 30 days. An example may be viewed at: www.cio.ost.dot.gov/policy/dirmm/DOT H1350.254.htm	*Addresses the subset of an organization's missions that are deemed most critical; usually written at headquarters level; not IT focused*
Incident Response Plan	Define strategies to detect, respond to, and limit consequences of malicious cyber incident. An example may be viewed at: www.fedcirc.gov/library/documents/82-02-70.pdf (requires Adobe Reader)	*Focuses on information security responses to incidents affecting systems and/or networks*
Occupant Emergency Plan (OEP)	Provide coordinated procedures for minimizing loss of life or injury and protecting property damage in response to a physical threat. An example may be viewed at: www.usda.gov/oo/beprepared?OEPplans.htm	*Focuses on personnel and property particular to the specific facility; not business process or IT system functionality based*

THE PLANNING STEPS YOU WILL TAKE WITH THIS BOOK

This book and accompanying CD-ROM focuses on helping you develop a comprehensive Business Continuity Plan that includes:

• Procedures for sustaining essential business operations while recovering from a significant disruption — Business Continuity Plan (BCP).

•   Procedures for recovering business operations immediately following a disaster — Business Recovery (or Resumption) Plan (BRP).

•   Procedures to facilitate recovery capabilities at an alternate data site — Disaster Recovery Plan (DRP).

> Note: The planning steps include the key elements listed below. More than one planning step may be covered within a chapter. So for ease of use and reference, the step being discussed will be shown at the bottom of each page.

Planning Steps

1.   Writing the Purpose, Objectives, Scope and Assumptions

2.   Choosing Your Plan Coordinator and Development Team

3.   Assigning Action Items, Coordination Responsibilities and Time Frames

4.   Doing Your Risk Assessment

5.   Doing Your Business Impact Analysis

6.   Selecting Your Recovery Teams

7.   Developing Your Recovery Strategies and Action Plans

8.   Documenting Your Business Continuity Plan

9.   Testing Your Plan

10.   Distributing Your Plan

11.   Maintaining Your Plan

STEP 1 — WRITING THE PURPOSE, OBJECTIVES, SCOPE AND ASSUMPTIONS

In Step 1 you will begin by writing the purpose, objectives, scope, and any assumptions you are making during plan development. Worksheets for each topic are on the CD-ROM along with sample text.

Purpose of the Plan — Sample Text

The purpose of this Business Continuity Plan is to provide for the continuation of critical business functions and recovery in the event of a disaster. Many potential contingencies and disasters can be averted, or the damage they cause can be reduced, if appropriate steps are taken to manage through the event.

This completed Business Continuity Plan outlines the course of action to be taken in the event of an emergency and the process for each business unit to follow in their recovery to normal business operations. It is intended to:

- Provide an orderly and efficient transition from normal to emergency conditions.

- Provide specific guidelines appropriate for complex and unpredictable occurrences.

- Provide consistency in action.

- Prevent activity inconsistent with the philosophy of our company.

- Establish a threshold at which an emergency response is triggered and determines who in the various locations may authorize the response.

Since all disasters tend to be unique, this plan will not address any one type of disaster nor define a specific recovery strategy for all possibilities. It is the purpose of this document to plan for the worst-case scenario, and therefore provide measures applicable to any situation. The intended use of this Business Continuity Plan is to minimize the impact of any unexpected occurrence causing a disruption in our company's critical business functions. The appendices contain information concerning equipment and inventory, the names and numbers of business contacts, suppliers, users and civil authorities that will need to be contacted.

Plan Objectives — Guidelines

The objectives of your Business Continuity Plan are typically to provide a level of security and safety for the people on the premises at the time of the disaster; minimize financial loss to your company; continue to serve your customers; and, mitigate the negative effects disruptions can have on your company's strategic plans, reputation, operations, liquidity, credit quality, market positions, and ability to remain in compliance with applicable laws and regulations.

Other typical objectives of Business Continuity Planning are:

- Continue critical business operations.

- Minimize the risk of delay in setting up an alternate business location.

- Minimize the duration of a serious disruption to business operations.

- Minimize immediate damage and loss.

- Establish management succession and emergency powers.

- Identify critical lines of business and supporting functions.

- Provide effective coordination of recovery tasks and reduce the complexity of the recovery effort.

- Provide a standard for testing the Business Continuity Plan.

- Minimize the decision making process during a disaster.

- Protect the shareholder's interest (if applicable).

- Manage successfully through a disaster.

- Receive positive media coverage as a result of advanced planning.

> *Note: As you work through the process, come back to your objectives to make adjustments in them as you find they are needed and to make sure you are staying true to them.*

Scope of the Plan - Guidelines

Historically, the data processing department has been assigned the duty of developing the Business Continuity Plan. Frequently, this has led to the development of plans to restore computer resources in a manner that is not fully responsive to the broader needs of the business. An enterprise-wide plan must include all critical business functions outside data processing. Business Continuity Planning is a *business* issue not just a data processing issue.

All disasters are possible. Companies in Florida tend to plan for hurricanes and power outages, those in California for earthquakes, those in the Midwest for tornadoes. September 11th made it clear that any kind of disaster is possible, anywhere. Therefore, it may be wise to plan for the impact of an outage rather than what caused it.

Planning for a single type of scenario may blind-side you to events of lower probability. It is far better to have the capability to contend with the worst disruption imaginable and then consider activities that may be required for lesser situations.

Scenarios to consider:

- The primary facility is destroyed

- Critical buildings, facilities, or geographic regions are not accessible

- Vendor assistance or service provider is not available

- Utilities are not available (power, telecommunications, etc.)

- Access to information resources (systems, networks, data) is lost

•   Critical documentation and/or records are not available

•   Skilled or key personnel, who perform critical processes, are not available

The most common approach is single building disasters. However, the nature of your facility and geographical location may warrant added alternatives beyond the single-building concept. For example, if your complex covers several acres or has more than one building and you are in an earthquake or flood zone, you may want to develop a Business Continuity Plan for the entire complex.

In addition, the September 11 terrorist incidents point out the risks related to your being in close proximity to likely terrorist targets and how destruction might affect the telecommunications, power, and transportation infrastructure you depend upon.

Planning Assumptions— Guidelines

The purpose of this planning function is to define the assumptions you make during plan development. It is quite likely that your initial assumptions will change as your plan progresses.

Carefully consider the assumptions on which the BCP is based. For example, you probably should not assume a disaster would be limited to a single facility or to a small geographic area. Nor should you assume that you will be able to gain access to facilities that have not been damaged, nor that critical personnel (including senior management) will be available immediately after the disruption. Assuming public transportation systems such as airlines, railroads and subways will be operating may also be incorrect.

General Examples

•   The type of disaster (fire, civil unrest, natural disaster, terrorist attack, chemical spill) and the impact of a disaster will vary significantly.

•   The Business Continuity Plan will be kept up-to-date and stored in a safe place.

•   Backups of software applications and data files necessary for recovery will be available at an off-site storage facility.

•   Copies of the Business Continuity Plan will be available (your locations) and/or with (your employee name/s, and/or on the Internet.

•   Contracted alternate sites will be available at the time of need.

•   Telecommunications needs have already been established and contracted for in advance.

•   A minimum staff will be available to perform critical functions of the plan.

•   Computer center equipment, including components supporting (system name), are connected to an uninterruptible power supply (UPS) that provides 45 minutes to 1 hour of electricity during a power failure.

- The equipment, connections and capabilities required to operate are available at the Alternate Site in *City, State*.

- Service agreements are maintained for hardware, software and communications providers to support the recovery.

- Managers will keep all personnel affected by this plan aware of its current procedures and practices

- All personnel must react quickly and effectively during the recovery process

- This plan will be maintained in accordance with the Maintenance & Testing Section.

- The Risk Management Department will perform the following tasks:

  1. Ensure employee safety.

  2. Communicate the event to the media, customers and vendors.

  3. Notify the police, fire department and civil authorities as needed.

  4. Communicate the event to the Insurance provider.

- A disaster will be declared and data processing will be moved to the recovery site when the outage is expected to exceed 24 hours.

STEP 2 — THE PLAN COORDINATOR AND DEVELOPMENT TEAM: JOB DESCRIPTIONS

This author assumes that your management has designated a Project Leader to begin developing a Business Continuity Plan. It is not uncommon for this same person to also be the Plan Coordinator. Whichever the case, it is important that the coordinator has experience in managing large projects, has an understanding of the company's business operations, and an appreciation for the interdependency between the data center and other departments.

The Plan Coordinator may also be responsible for the plan's maintenance. This includes ensuring that all revisions are made, documented, and remains relative to other plans when multiple plans are developed, for example: an Occupant Emergency Plan.

The Plan Development Team

Having secured the commitment of senior management and department managers, selection of the team members by the Project Leader or Plan Coordinator may begin. The makeup of the team will vary depending upon the size of your organization and the number of departments involved. Determine who can be an active member and who can serve in an advisory capacity. In most cases, one or two people will be doing most of the work. At the very least, obtain input from all functional areas. Remember these:

- Facilities/Security

- Customer Service

- Human Resources

- Sales and Marketing

- Data Processing and Operations

- Legal

- Telecommunications and networks

- Data Entry

- Data Security

- Finance and purchasing

- Administration/Contracts

- Systems and Applications programming

- Production Control

- Public Information Officer

- Community relations

- Upper management

- Line management

- Labor

- Engineering and maintenance

Each member of the Plan Development Team will be assigned the following in Step 3.

- Primary Actions Items; and,

- Coordination Responsibilities.

For now, use the *Plan Development Team Roster* found in Worksheet 1 to list your permanent "Development Team" participants. Use Worksheet 1.1 for those members who will be participating in an advisory capacity.

Worksheet 1

Plan Development Team Roster

	Department and Title	Contact Phone Numbers	E-Mail/Comments
1			
2			
3			
4			
5			
6			
7			
8			
9			

Worksheet 1.1

Plan Development Team Roster — As-Needed Basis

	Department and Title	Contact Phone Numbers	E-Mail/Comments
1.			
2.			
3.			
4.			
5.			
6.			
7.			
8.			
9.			

STEP 3 — ASSIGNING ACTION ITEMS, COORDINATION OF RESPONSIBILITIES AND TIMEFRAMES

Having identified the plan development team responsible for creating the Plan (Step 2), it is now time to begin identifying the action items and coordination responsibilities for each team member. Assign each responsibility to only one person with an estimate of hours required for completion. More than one person working on a task is fine, as long as the ultimate responsibility is in the hands of only one.

> Note: The plan's purpose, objectives, scope, and assumptions (Step 1), should be reviewed with the project team and modified as needed. If these items are not completed, finalize them during the first or second team meeting.

Before beginning Step 3, select the Plan Coordinator and/or Project Leader. This can be a temporary role, but a better approach would be for this to be a permanent role even if considered a part-time responsibility once the final BCP is in place.

The BCP Plan Coordinator should possess good leadership qualities, a good understanding of business processes and business management, experience in IT and information security, and strong project management capabilities. Ideally, this person would be known and respected by all the company departments with which he/she must work to create the plan. This person is far more likely to receive cooperation from others if there is already some positive relationship on which to depend. You may also want to look into purchasing business continuity planning software. There are a number of good programs available and they could make the Plan Coordinator's job go that much smoother.

Once the coordinator has been selected, this individual will convene the team members and introduce (or develop) the purpose of the project, its objectives, scope, planning assumptions and targeted completion date. If a completion date has not been specified, set a realistic target date based on the complexity of your action items. Assuming the tasks for the first meeting have been accomplished and documented, you are ready to begin developing your work plan by assigning action items and responsibilities. The work plan should contain target and actual completion dates for each item. After you have developed the project work plan, verify that a complete business continuity and recovery plan will result from your following it.

Bear in mind that the project timeframe is going to depend upon:

- The size of your organization - the more departments and staff who must participate, the greater and more complex the task.

- The complexity of your critical business functions - if the major activities of your company are straightforward and do not require complex procedures or information, the creation of the BCP should not take as long.

- The support of senior management to reach across departmental boundaries to get the job done.

- Good and regular communication regarding the plan's progress - from management to staff, from plan coordinator to staff and management, from group to group among the staff.

- A dedicated staff to conduct the activities of the business continuity program, even if it is a part-time responsibility.

On Worksheet 2, the *Project Planning Guideline* for developing an action item list is shown. The guideline covers the steps taken in this book (Steps 1 thru 11) with a reference to the chapter number where the planning steps are discussed in more detail. If Business Continuity Planning is new to you, please read all the steps in this book prior to developing your project plan. The review will help you better understand the planning process, its scope, and various recovery solutions that need to be considered.

> *Note: Your project plan ultimately becomes the foundation of your recovery plan, so be sure to include all the action items necessary for total business resumption.*

Worksheet 2

Project Planning Schedule

Action Items, Coordination of Responsibilities & Time Frames

Action Item	Action Item Coordinator	Targeted Completion	Actual Completion	Comments or Cross Reference to the Generated Plan Outline
DEFINE PLAN OBJECTIVES, IDENTIFY THE PLAN DEVELOPMENT TEAM AND OBTAIN MANAGEMENT SIGN-OFF. *(Action items should cover Steps 1 & 2. See Chapter 1 for details.)*				
1. Finalize and document the plan's purpose, scope, objectives and assumptions				
2. Finalize and document the Plan Development Team roster				
3. Appoint a plan coordinator and/or project leader				

Action Item	Action Item Coordinator	Targeted Completion	Actual Completion	Comments or Cross Reference to the Generated Plan Outline
4. Convene the team to assign action items, responsibilities and targeted completion date				
5. Determine a targeted completion date for the final document				
6. Secure management sign-off on the plan's scope, purpose, objectives, assumptions and targeted completion date				
ANALYZE CAPABILITIES AND HAZARDS *(Step 4. See Chapter 3 for details)*				
1. Review Internal Plans and Policies:(Where do we stand right now?) — evacuation plan, fire protection plan, safety and health program, etc.				
2. Meet with outside government agencies, community organizations and utilities. (Learn about potential emergencies and available resources for responding to them)				
3. Identify applicable Federal, State, and Local regulations such as: fire codes, seismic safety codes, etc.				
4. Identify internal resources and capabilities; personnel, equipment, backup systems, etc.				

Action Item	Action Item Coordinator	Targeted Completion	Actual Completion	Comments or Cross Reference to the Generated Plan Outline
5. Identify external resources (local emergency management office, fire department, hazardous materials response organizations, etc.				
6. Assess the vulnerability of our facility, the probability and potential impact of each hazard we identify: • Assess the potential business impact. • Secure budget approval from management for risk mitigation.				
CONDUCT BUSINESS IMPACT ANALYSIS FOR COMPUTER DEPENDENT FUNCTIONS *(Step 5. See Chapter 3 for sample questionnaire and evaluation tools.)*				
1. Define critical business functions and related computer systems needing protection.				
2. Interview IT and end user personnel to identify critical software applications, systems and resources managed by the IT Department.				

Action Item	Action Item Coordinator	Targeted Completion	Actual Completion	Comments or Cross Reference to the Generated Plan Outline
3. Assemble information gathered and document the resources needed for recovery. Include: • required hardware, software and databases • critical forms, supplies • key personnel and backups • vendor lists				
4. Analyze results and prioritize the functions needing protection				
5. Identify critical software applications to be supported. • Class 1 – essential to business survival • Class 2 – to be recovered after • Class 3 – will not be available during recovery operation				
6. Assemble information and document the computer room recovery strategy for each department.				
7. Prepare Business Impact Analysis Report				

Action Item	Action Item Coordinator	Targeted Completion	Actual Completion	Comments or Cross Reference to the Generated Plan Outline
DEVELOP CRITICAL RECORDS BACKUP AND RECOVERY PROCEDURES *(Step 5. See Chapter 3 for suggested guidelines.)*				
1. Determine records requiring protection				
2. Select an off-site storage facility for critical records and applications				
3. Develop a backup policy				
4. Develop an off-site storage policy. Include: • applications and data recovery procedures • off-site storage notification procedures				
5. Implement the backup policy				
6. Implement the off-site storage policy; obtain vendor's commitment in writing.				
7. Test the vital records restoration procedure				
IDENTIFY RECOVERY TEAMS AND ALTERNATE PROCESSING SITE *(Step 6. See Chapter 3 for suggested guidelines)*				
1. Document all resources needed to recover. (Hot sites, cold sites, mobile shells, recovery teams, etc.)				

Action Item	Action Item Coordinator	Targeted Completion	Actual Completion	Comments or Cross Reference to the Generated Plan Outline
2. Review alternate processing locations to determine their adequacy to meet requirements				
3. Select an alternate site				
4. Obtain vendor commitment in writing				
WRITE THE EMERGENCY ACTION PLANS *(Step 7. See Chapter 3 "Sample Action Plan Task List")*				
1. Write an emergency action plan for each critical application determined by the Business Impact Analysis Report. Note: More than one person may be needed to complete this item				
WRITE AND MAINTAIN THE PLAN *(Steps 8 & 11. See Chapters 4 & 5 for suggested guidelines)*				
1. Assemble information gathered from the project members				
2. Develop a plan outline for organizing the continuity plan. (Can be used later as the table of contents)				
3. Document the information gathered				
4. Review draft with project team				
5. Obtain project team and department head sign-off.				

Action Item	Action Item Coordinator	Targeted Completion	Actual Completion	Comments or Cross Reference to the Generated Plan Outline
6. Develop procedures for maintaining the plan				
7. Obtain senior management sign-off.				
TEST THE PLAN *(Step 9. See Chapter 5 for testing guidelines)*				
1. Train recovery teams, managers and staff				
2. Coordinate testing activities to ensure the adequacy of action plan(s)				
3. Identify deficiencies in action plan(s)				
4. Modify existing plan as needed based on test results				
5. Obtain management sign-off				
6. Develop the Plan Distribution List				
7. Develop Plan Maintenance Procedures.				

..

BY KENNETH L. FULMER

3

ITS TIME TO ROLL UP YOUR SLEEVES AND TO ASSESS YOUR CURRENT RISK

This chapter explains the Risk Assessment and Analysis, and the importance of conducting it early in the planning process. The Risk Analysis section is then followed by a discussion of the Business Impact Analysis (BIA), its purpose and how to accomplish the task. The final section of this chapter provides guidelines developing recovery strategies and team selection.

By the end of this chapter you will have:

- Identified your current capabilities and vulnerabilities

- Identified your critical business functions, applications and vital records

- Developed your Recovery Strategies and Action Plans

- Selected your Recovery Teams

- Have completed Steps 4 thru 7: Where Do You Stand Right Now? Accessing Your Risk; Doing Your Business Impact Analysis; Selecting Your Recovery Teams; and, Developing Your Recovery Strategies and Action Plans.

STEP 4 — WHERE DO YOU STAND RIGHT NOW?

Although the exact nature of potential disasters and their impacts on your business is impossible to determine, the benefits derived from assessing potential emergencies and then eliminating or mitigating those that your business cannot tolerate is obvious. Since the purpose of your Business Continuity Plan is to ensure the safety of staff and company assets, the Risk Assessment and Analysis should be performed early in your planning process, so that easily rectifiable hazards can be eliminated as soon as possible.

While preventive measures can quickly reduce exposure to many risks, there will be those risks that are more difficult to eliminate or impossible for you to prevent like wars, terrorist attacks and natural disasters. Now you must determine how much risk your business is willing to tolerate and at what point it must respond quickly and effectively. Remember, since all disasters tend to be unique, you cannot define a strategy for all the possibilities. Many companies will choose to plan for the worst-case scenario, and therefore provide measures applicable to most any situation.

It is now important to find out what your current capabilities are for dealing with emergencies and what potential hazards may be located near your facility of which you are unaware.

Begin by Reviewing Internal Plans and Policies

Documents to look for include:

- Evacuation plan

- Fire protection plan

- Safety and health program

- Environmental policies

- Security procedures

- Insurance program

- Finance and purchasing procedures

- Plant closing policy

- Employee manuals

- Hazardous materials plan

- Process safety assessment

- Risk management plan

- Capital improvement program

- Mutual aid agreements

Meet with Outside Groups

Meet with government agencies, communication organizations and utilities. Ask about potential emergencies and about plans and available resources for responding to them. Sources of information include:

- Community emergency management office

- Mayor or Community Administrator's office

- Local Emergency Planning Committee (LEPC)

- Fire Department

- Police Department

- Emergency Medical Services organizations

- American Red Cross

- National Weather Service

- Public Works Department

> *Note: While researching potential emergencies, one facility discovered a dam – 50 miles away – posed a threat to its community. The facility was able to plan accordingly.*

- Planning Commission

- Telephone Companies

- Electric Utilities

- Neighboring businesses

Identify Codes and Regulations

Identify applicable Federal, State and local regulations such as:

- Occupational safety and health regulations

- Environmental regulations

- Fire codes

- Seismic safety codes

- Transportation regulations

- Zoning regulations

- Corporate policies

Identify Critical Products, Services and Operations

You will need this information to assess the impact of potential emergencies and to determine the need for backup systems. Areas to review include:

- Company products and services and the facilities and equipment needed to produce them.

- Products and services provided by suppliers, especially sole source providers.

- Lifeline services such as electric power, water, sewer, gas, telecommunications and transportation

- Operations, equipment and personnel vital to the continued functioning of the facility.

Identify Your Internal Resources and Capabilities

Resources and capabilities that could be needed in an emergency include:

- **Personnel** — fire brigades, hazardous materials response team, emergency medical services, security, emergency management group, evacuation team, public information officer.

- **Equipment** — fire protection and suppression equipment, communications equipment, first aid supplies, emergency supplies, warning systems, emergency power equipment, and decontamination equipment.

- **Facilities** — emergency operating center, media briefing area, shelter area, first-aid stations, sanitation facilities

- **Organizational capabilities** — training, evacuation plan, employee support system

- **Backup systems** — arrangements with other facilities to provide for:

  1. Payroll

  2. Communications

  3. Production

  4. Customer services

  5. Shipping and receiving

  6. Information systems support

  7. Emergency power

  8. Recovery support

Identify External Resources

There are many external resources that could be needed in an emergency. In some cases, formal agreements may be necessary to define your facility's relationship with the following:

- Local emergency management office

- Fire Department

- Hazardous materials response organization

- Emergency medical services

- Hospitals

- Local and State police

- Community service organizations

- Utilities

- Contractors

- Suppliers of emergency equipment

- Insurance carriers

Conduct an Insurance Review

Many companies discover that they are not properly insured, only after they have suffered a loss. Lack of appropriate insurance can be financially devastating. Discuss the following topics with your insurance advisor to determine your individual needs.

- How will our property be valued?

- Does our policy cover the cost of required upgrades to code?

- How much insurance are we required to carry to avoid becoming a co-insurer?

- What perils or causes of loss does our policy cover?

- What are our deductibles?

- Is coverage for replacement cost, depreciated value, or original cost?

- What does our policy require us to do in the event of loss?

- What types of records and documentation will the insurance company want to see? Are records in a safe place where they can be obtained after an emergency?

- To what extent are we covered for loss due to interruption of power? Is coverage provided for both on- and off-premises power interruption?

- Are we covered for lost income in the event of business interruption? Do we have enough coverage? How long is our coverage for lost income if the business is closed by order of a civil authority?

- To what extent are we covered for reduced income due to customers not all immediately coming back once the business reopens?

- How will our emergency management program affect our rates?

Assess Your Vulnerability

You are now ready to begin assessing the vulnerability of your facility — the probability and the potential impact of each emergency. Use the "Vulnerability Analysis Chart" on Worksheet 3 to help you through this process. This entails your assigning probabilities, estimating impact and assessing your resources using a numerical system. The lower the score the better.

In the first column of the chart, list all the emergencies that could affect you facility, including those identified by you local emergency management office.

If your Risk Assessment is for the data center only, you may want to consider using the alternative Risk Assessment Template and Risk Analysis Checklist, Appendices A and B.

> Note: Whichever template you choose to follow, you must tailor your Project Planning Schedule accordingly — Worksheet 2.

Begin by Listing Potential Threats

- Threats that could occur within your facility

- Threats that could occur in your community

Below are some other factors to consider.

- **Historical** — What types of emergencies have already occurred in your community, at your facility or at other facilities in the area?

    - Fires

    - Severe weather

    - Hazardous material spills

    - Biological incident

    - Transportation accidents

    - Utility outages

    - Earthquakes, hurricanes, tornadoes

    - Terrorism

- **Geographical** — What can happen as a result of your facility's location? Keep in mind:

    - Proximity to flood plains, seismic faults and dams

    - Proximity to companies that produce, store, use or transport hazardous materials

    - Proximity to nuclear power plants

    - Major transportation routes and airports

- **Technological** — What could result from a process or system failure? Possibilities include:

    - Fire, explosion, hazardous materials incident

    - Safety system failure

    - Telecommunications failure

    - Computer system failure

    - Power failure

    - Heating/cooling system failure

    - Emergency notification system failure

- **Human Error** — What emergencies could be caused by employee error? Are your employees trained to work safely? Do they know what to do in an emergency?

    - Human error is the single largest cause of workplace emergencies and can result from:

    - Poor training

    - Poor maintenance

    - Carelessness

    - Misconduct

    - Substance abuse

    - Fatigue

- **Physical** — What types of emergencies could result from the design or construction of your facility? Does the physical facility enhance safety? Consider:

    - The physical construction of your facility

    - Hazardous processes or by-products

    - Facilities for storing combustibles

    - Layout of equipment

    - Lighting

- • Evacuation routes and exits

- • Proximity of shelter area

- **Regulatory** — What emergencies or hazards are you regulated to deal with? Analyze each potential emergency from beginning to end. Consider what could happen as a result of:

  - • Prohibited access to the facility

  - • Loss of electric power

  - • Communication lines down

  - • Ruptured gas mains

  - • Water damage

  - • Smoke damage

  - • Structural damage

  - • Air or waster contamination

  - • Explosion

  - • Building collapse

  - • Trapped persons

  - • Chemical release

Estimate Probability

Assign a rating in the Probability column of the *Vulnerability Analysis Chart* rating the likelihood of each emergency's occurrence. This is a subjective consideration, but useful nonetheless.

Use a simple scale of 1 to 5 with 1 as the lowest probability and 5 as the highest.

Assess the Potential Human Impact

Analyze the potential human impact of each emergency — the possibility of death or injury.

Assign a rating in the Human Impact column of the *Vulnerability Analysis Chart*. Use 1 as the lowest impact and 5 as the highest.

> *Note: One bank's risk analysis concluded that a "small" fire could be as catastrophic to the business as a computer system failure. The planning team discovered that the bank employees did not know how to use the fire extinguishers, and that the bank lacked any kind of evacuation or emergency response system.*

Assess the Potential Property Impact

Consider the potential property for losses and damages. Again, assign a rating in the Property Impact column, 1 being the lowest impact and 5 being the highest. Consider:

- Cost to replace

- Cost to set up temporary replacement

- Cost to repair

Assess the Potential Business Impact

Consider the potential loss of market share. Assign a rating in the Business Impact Column. Again, assign 1 for the lowest impact and 5 for the highest.

- Assess the impact of:

- Business interruption

- Employees unable to report to work

- Customers unable to reach your facility

- Company in violation of contractual agreements

- Imposition of fines and penalties or legal costs

- Interruption of critical supplies

- Interruption of product distribution

Assess Internal and External Resources

Next, assess your resources and ability to respond. Assign a score to your Internal Resources and External Resources. The lower the score, the better.

To help you do this, consider each potential emergency from beginning to end and each resource that would be needed to respond. For each emergency, ask these questions:

- Will we have the needed resources and capabilities to respond if key employees, contractors, vendors, etc., are not available?

- For this emergency, will external resources be able to respond to us as quickly as we may need them, or will they have other priority areas to serve?

If the answers are yes, move on to the next assessment. If the answers are no, identify what can be done to correct the problem. For example, you may need to:

- Develop additional emergency procedures

- Conduct additional training

- Acquire additional equipment

- Establish mutual aid agreements

- Establish agreements with specialized contractors

> *Note: When assessing resources, remember that community emergency workers — police, paramedics and firefighters — will focus their response where the need is greatest. Or, they may be victims themselves and not be able to respond immediately. That means response to your facility may be delayed.*

Add the Columns

Total the scores for each emergency. The lower the score, the better. While this is a subjective rating, the comparisons will help determine planning and resource priorities. Some of the more common hazards are listed on the following page, plus planning considerations for each.

HAZARD-SPECIFIC INFORMATION

This section provides information about some of the most common hazards:

- Fire

- Hazardous Material Incidents

- Floods and Flash Floods

- Hurricanes

- Tornadoes

- Severe Winter Storms

- Earthquakes

- Technological Emergencies

- Fire: Fire is the most common of all the hazards. Every year fire causes thousands of deaths and injuries and billions of dollars in property damage.

Planning Considerations

Consider the following when developing your plan:

- Research fire codes and regulations required by the Occupational Safety and Health Administration (OSHA, www.osha.gov) and The National Fire Protection Association (www.nfpa.org).

- Meet with the fire department to talk about the community's fire response capabilities.

- Ask your insurance carrier to recommend fire prevention and protection measures. Your carrier may also offer training.

- Distribute fire safety information to employees: how to prevent fires in the workplace, how to contain a fire, how to evacuate the facility, where to report a fire.

- Instruct personnel to use the stairs — not elevators — in a fire. Instruct them to crawl on their hands and knees when escaping a hot or smoke-filled area.

- Conduct evacuation drills. Post maps of evacuation routes in prominent places. Keep evacuation routes including stairways and doorways clear of debris.

- Assign fire wardens for each area to monitor shutdown and evacuation procedures.

- Establish procedures for the safe handling and storage of flammable liquids and gases and procedures to prevent the accumulation of combustible materials.

- Provide for the safe disposal of smoking materials.

- Establish a preventive maintenance schedule to keep equipment operating safely.

- Place fire extinguishers in appropriate locations.

- Train employees in use of fire extinguishers.

- Install smoke detectors. Check smoke detectors once a month, change batteries at least once a year.

- Establish a system for warning personnel of a fire. Consider installing a fire alarm with automatic notification to the fire department.

- Consider installing a sprinkler system, fire hoses and fire-resistant walls and doors.

- Ensure that key personnel are familiar with all fire safety systems.

- Identify and mark all utility shut offs so that fire wardens or responding personnel can shut off electric power, gas or water quickly.

- Determine the level of response your facility will need if a fire occurs. Among the options are:

  - *Option 1* — Immediate evacuation of all personnel on alarm.

  - *Option 2* — All personnel are trained in fire extinguisher use. Personnel in the immediate area of a fire attempt to control it. If they cannot, the fire alarm is sounded and all personnel evacuate.

  - *Option 3* — Only designated personnel are trained in fire extinguisher use.

  - *Option 4* — A fire team is trained to fight first-stage fires than can be controlled without protective equipment or breathing apparatus. Beyond this level fire, the team evacuates.

- Option 5 — A fire team is trained and equipped to fight structural fires using protective equipment and breathing apparatus.

Hazardous Materials Incidents

Hazardous materials are substances that are flammable or combustible, explosive, toxic, noxious, corrosive, oxidizable, an irritant, or radioactive. A hazardous material spill or release can pose a risk to life, health or property. An incident can result in the evacuation of a few people, a section of a facility or an entire neighborhood.

There are a number of Federal laws that regulate hazardous materials, including: the Superfund Amendments and Reauthorization Act of 1986 (SARA), and Resource Conservation and Recovery Act of 1976 (RCRA), the Hazardous Materials Transportation Act (HMTA), the Occupational Safety and Health Act (OSHA), the Toxic Substances Control Act (TSCA) and the Clean Air Act.

Title III of SARA regulates the packaging, labeling, handling, storage and transportation of hazardous materials. The law requires facilities to furnish information about the quantities and health effects of materials used at the facility, and to promptly notify local and State officials whenever a significant release of hazardous materials occurs.

In addition to on-site hazards, be aware of the potential for an off-site incident affecting your operations.

Also, be aware of hazardous materials used in facility processes and in the construction of the physical plant.

Detailed definitions as well as lists of hazardous materials can be obtained from the Environmental Protection Agency (EPA), and the Occupational Safety and Health Administration (OSHA).

Planning Considerations

Consider the following when developing your plan:

- Identify and label all hazardous materials stored, handled produced and disposed of by your facility. Follow government regulations that apply to your facility. Obtain material safety data sheets (MSDS) for all hazardous materials at your location.

- Ask the local fire department for assistance in developing appropriate response procedures.

- Train employees to recognize and report hazardous material spills and releases. Train employees in proper handling and storage.

- Establish procedures to notify management and emergency response organizations of an incident.

- Establish procedures to warn employees of an incident.

- Establish evacuation procedures

- Depending on your operations, organize and train an emergency response team to confine and control hazardous material spills in accordance with applicable regulations.

- Identify other facilities in your area that use hazardous materials. Determine whether an incident could affect your facility.

- Identify highways, railroads and waterways near your facility used for the transportation of hazardous materials.

- Determine how a transportation accident near your facility could affect your operation.

Floods and Flash Floods

Floods are the most common and widespread of all natural disasters. Most communities in the United States can experience some degree of flooding after spring rains, heavy thunderstorms or winter snow thaws.

Most floods develop slowly over a period of days. Flash floods, however, are like walls of water that develop in a matter of minutes. Flash floods can be caused by intense storms or dam failure.

Planning Considerations

Consider the following when preparing for floods:

- Ask you local emergency management office whether your facility is located in a flood plain. Learn the history of flooding in your area. Learn the elevation of your facility in relation to streams, rivers and dams.

• Review the community's emergency plan. Learn the community's evacuation routes. Know where to find higher ground in case of a flood.

• Establish warning and evacuation procedures for the facility. Make plans for assisting employees who may need transportation.

• Inspect areas in your facility subject to flooding. Identify records and equipment that can be moved to a higher location. Make plans to move records and equipment in case of flood.

• Purchase an NOAA Weather Radio with a warning alarm tone and battery backup. Listen for flood watches and warnings.

  • *Flood Watch* — Flooding is possible. Stay tuned to NOAA radio. Be prepared to evacuate. Tune to local radio and television stations for additional information.

  • *Flood Warning* — Flooding is already occurring or will occur soon. Take precautions at once. Be prepared to go to higher ground. If advised, evacuate immediately.

  • Ask your insurance carrier for information about flood insurance. Regular property and casualty insurance generally does not cover flooding.

• Consider the feasibility of flood proofing your facility. There are three basic types of methods

  1. Permanent flood-proofing measures are taken before a flood occurs and require no human intervention when flood waters rise. They include:

    a) Filling windows, doors or other openings with water-resistant materials such as concrete blocks or bricks. This approach assumes the structure is strong enough to withstand floodwaters.

    b) Installing check valves to prevent water from entering where utility and sewer lines enter the facility.

    c) Reinforcing walls to resist water pressure. Sealing walls to prevent or reduce seepage.

    d) Building watertight walls around equipment or work areas within the facility that are particularly susceptible to flood damage.

    e) Constructing flood walls or levees outside the facility to keep flood waters away.

    f) Elevating the facility on walls, columns or compacted fill. This approach is most applicable to new construction, though many types of buildings can be elevated.

  2. Contingency flood proofing measurers are also taken before a flood but require some additional action when flooding occurs. These measurers include:

    a) Installing watertight barriers called flood shields to prevent the passage of water through doors, windows, ventilation shafts or other openings.

    b) Installing permanent watertight doors.

c)   Installing permanent pumps to remove floodwaters.

3. Emergency flood proofing measurer are generally less expensive than those listed above, though they require substantial advanced warning and do not satisfy the minimum requirements for watertight flood proofing as set forth by the National Flood Insurance Program (NFIP). They include:

a)   Building walls with sandbags.

b)   Constructing a double row of walls with boards and posts to create a "crib," then filling the crib with soil.

c)   Constructing a single wall by stacking small beams or planks on top of each other.

- Consider the need for backup systems:

  - Portable pumps to remove floodwater.

  - Alternate power sources such as generators or gasoline-powered pumps.

  - Battery-powered emergency lighting.

- Participate in community flood control projects.

Hurricanes

Hurricanes are severe tropical storms with sustained winds of 74 miles per hour or greater. Their winds can reach 160 miles per hour and extend inland for hundreds of miles.

Hurricanes bring torrential rains and a storm surge of ocean water that crashes into land as the storm approaches. Hurricanes also spawn tornadoes.

The National Weather Service issues hurricane advisories as soon as a hurricane appears to be a threat. The hurricane season lasts from June through November.

Planning Considerations

The following are considerations when preparing for hurricanes:

- Ask your local emergency management office about community evacuation plans.

- Establish facility shutdown procedures. Establish warning and evacuation procedures. Make plans for assisting employees who may need transportation.

- Make plans for communicating with employees' families before and after the hurricane.

- Purchase an NOAA Weather Radio with a warning alarm tone and battery backup. List for hurricane watches and warnings.

  - *Hurricane Watch* — A hurricane is possible within 24 to 36 hours. Stay tuned for additional advisories. Tune to local radio and television stations for additional information. An evacuation may be necessary.

- *Hurricane Warning* — A hurricane will hit land within 24 hours. Take precautions at once. If advised, evacuate immediately.

- Survey your facility. Make plans to protect outside equipment and structures.

- Make plans to protect windows. Permanent storm shutters offer the best protection. Covering windows with 5/8" marine plywood is a second option.

    - Consider the need for backup systems:

    - Portable pumps to remove floodwater

    - Alternate power sources such as generators or gasoline-powered pumps

    - Battery-powered emergency lighting.

- Prepare to move records, computers and other items within your facility or to another location.

Tornadoes

Tornadoes are extremely violent local storms that extend to the ground with whirling winds that can reach 300 mph.

Spawned from powerful thunderstorms, tornadoes can uproot trees and buildings and turn harmless objects into deadly missiles in a matter of seconds. Damage paths can be in excess of one mile wide and 50 miles long.

Tornadoes can occur in any state, but occur more frequently in the Midwest, Southeast and Southwest. They occur with little or no warning.

Planning Considerations

The following are considerations when preparing for hurricanes:

- Ask your local emergency management office about the community's tornado warning system.

- Purchase an NOAA Weather Radio with warning alarm tone and battery backup. Listen for tornado watches and warnings.

    - *Tornado Watch* — Tornadoes are likely. Be ready to take shelter. Stay tuned to radio and television stations for additional information.

    - *Tornado Warning* — A tornado has been sighted in the area or is indicated by radar. Take shelter immediately.

- Establish procedures to inform personnel when tornado warnings are posted. Consider the need for spotters to be responsible for looking out for approaching storms.

- Work with a structural engineer or architect to designate shelter areas in your facility. Ask your local emergency management office or National Weather Service office for guidance.

- Consider the amount of space you will need. Adults require about six square feet of space; nursing home and hospital patients require more.

- The best protection in a tornado is usually an underground area. If an underground area is not available, consider:

  - Small interior rooms on the lowest floor and without windows

  - Hallways on the lowest floor (format) away from doors and windows

  - Rooms constructed with reinforced concrete, brick or block with no windows and a heavy concrete floor or roof system overhead

> *Note: Auditoriums, cafeterias and gymnasiums that are covered with a flat, wide-span roof are not considered safe.*

- Make plans for evacuating personnel away from lightweight modular offices or mobile home-sized buildings. These structures offer no protection from tornadoes.

- Conduct tornado drills.

- Once in the shelter, personnel should protect their heads with arms and crouch down.

Severe Winter Storms

Severe winter storms bring heavy snow, ice, strong winds and freezing rain. Winter storms can prevent employees and customer from reaching the facility, leading to a temporary shutdown until roads are cleared. Heavy snow and ice can also cause structural damage and power outages.

Planning Considerations

Following are considerations for preparing for winter storms:

- Listen to NOAA Weather Radio and local radio and television stations for weather information:

  - *Winter Storm Watch* — Severe winter weather is possible.

  - *Winter Storm Warning* — Severe winter weather is expected.

  - *Blizzard Warning* — Severe winter weather with sustained winds of at least 35 mph is expected.

- *Traveler's Advisory* — Severe winter conditions may make driving difficult or dangerous.

- Establish procedures for facility shutdown and early release of employees.

- Store food, water, blankets, battery-powered radios with extra batteries and other emergency supplies for employees who become stranded at the facility.

- Provide a backup power source for critical operations.

- Arrange for snow and ice removal from parking lots, walkways, loading docks, etc.

Earthquakes

Earthquakes occur most frequently west of the Rocky Mountains, although historically the most violent earthquakes have occurred in the central United States. Earthquakes occur suddenly and without warning.

Earthquakes can seriously damage buildings and their contents; disrupt gas, electric and telephone services; and trigger landslides, avalanches, flash floods, fires and huge ocean waves called tsunamis. Aftershocks can occur for weeks following an earthquake.

In many buildings, the greatest danger to people in an earthquake is when equipment and non-structural elements such as ceilings, partitions, windows and lighting fixtures shake loose.

Planning Considerations

Following are guidelines for preparing for earthquakes:

- Assess your facility's vulnerability to earthquakes. Ask local government agencies for seismic information for your area.

- Have your facility inspected by a structural engineer. Develop and prioritize strengthening measures. These may include:

  - Adding steel bracing to frames

  - Adding shear walls to frames

  - Strengthening columns and building foundations

  - Replacing unreinforced brick filler walls

- Follow safety codes when constructing a facility or making major renovations.

- Inspect non-structural systems such as air conditioning, communications and pollution control systems. Assess the potential for damage. Prioritize measures to prevent damages.

- Inspect your facility for any item that could fall, spill, break or move during an earthquake. Take steps to reduce the following hazards:

- Move large and heavy objects to lower shelves or the floor. Hang heavy items away from where people work.

- Secure shelves, filing cabinets, tall furniture, desktop equipment, computers, printers, copiers and light fixtures.

- Secure fixed equipment and heavy machinery to the floor. Larger equipment can be placed on casters and attached to tethers that attach to the wall.

- Add bracing to suspended ceilings, if necessary.

- Install safety glass where appropriate.

- Secure large utility and process piping.

- Keep copies of design drawings of the facility to be used in assessing the facility's safety after an earthquake.

- Review processes for handling and storing hazardous materials. Have incompatible chemicals stored separately.

- Ask your insurance carrier about earthquake insurance and mitigation techniques.

- Establish procedures to determine whether an evacuation is necessary after an earthquake.

- Designate areas in the facility away from exterior walls and windows where occupants should gather after an earthquake if an evacuation is not necessary.

- Conduct earthquake drills. Provide personnel with the following safety information:

- In an earthquake, if indoors, stay there. Take cover under a sturdy piece of furniture or counter, or brace yourself against an inside wall or doorway. Protect your head and neck.

- If outdoors, move into the open, away from buildings, streetlights and utility wires.

- After an earthquake, stay away from windows, skylights and items that could fall. Do not use elevators.

- Use stairways to leave the building if it is determined that a building evacuation is necessary.

Technological Emergencies

Technological emergencies include any interruption or loss of a utility service, power source, life support system, information system or equipment needed to keep the business in operation.

Planning Considerations

The following are suggestions for planning for technological emergencies:

- Identify all critical operations, including:

    - Utilities including electric power, gas, water, hydraulics, compressed air, municipal and internal sewer systems, wastewater treatment services.

    - Security and alarm systems, elevators, lighting, life support systems, heating, ventilation and air conditioning systems, electrical distribution systems.

    - Manufacturing equipment, pollution control equipment.

    - Communication systems, both data and voice computer networks

    - Transportation systems including air, highway, railroad and waterway

- Determine the impact of service disruption.

- Ensure that key safety and maintenance personnel are thoroughly familiar with all building systems.

- Establish procedures for restoring systems. Determine need for backup systems.

- Establish preventive maintenance schedules for all systems and equipment

Analyzing the Risk Assessment

Review the results of your risk assessment and take immediate steps to minimize threats due to poor housekeeping habits, sporadic backup practices, obvious fire hazards, on-site storage of vital records, etc. By establishing these fundamental safeguards, you will reduce your vulnerability and be on your way to minimizing your company's exposure.

The next step in analyzing your risk assessment is to determine whether to accept or correct the other threats that are more costly to rectify. This decision usually involves senior management. It is important that management know what the risks are, what their probable consequences are, and what steps can be taken to cost-effectively avoid or minimize them. One of the best ways of providing this information to management is through an effective *Business Impact Analysis*.

Worksheet 3

Vulnerability Analysis Chart

Type of Emergency	Probability	Human Impact	Property Impact	Business Impact	Internal Resources	External Resources	Total Points
Examples	High		Low	Strong		Weak	
	5 ←→ 1			5 ←→ 1			
Fire	3	5	5	5	5	4	26
Severe Weather	5	5	5	4	3	3	25
Utility Outage	5	2	1	3	4	2	18

Note: The lower the score the better

STEP 5 — DOING YOUR BUSINESS IMPACT ANALYSIS

This report is normally based on questionnaires, interviews and the evaluation of information concerning critical business functions, computer usage, hardware and network configurations, vendors, critical applications, computer operations, site security and existing recovery procedures. If management requires, your report may also include recommendations on disaster recovery priorities, how recovery should be organized, what disaster backup options should be considered, recommendations for improving loss prevention and disaster preparedness, along with the cost and benefits of each recommendation.

The *Business Impact Report* should provide only the information needed to perform a convincing presentation to senior management that justifies the necessary funding for the Business Continuity Plan and associated services. You can scale down your BIA if the need for a plan has already been established, its funding approved and all critical business functions and systems identified.

Regardless of what situation you find yourself in, it is important to interview all the departments in your company. You may believe you know what is critical and what i's not, but in most cases when the interviewing process is skipped, something very important will fall through the cracks!

Software tools are available to help you with your BIA as well as for Business Continuity Planning. BIA software can help ensure that the assessment is accurate by reducing the opportunity for politics or bias to creep into the decision-making process. In addition, a BIA tool standardizes the process of collecting information from corporate-wide locations and on determining the importance management places on protecting each of these functions.

The following section, *Identifying Critical Systems, Applications and Vital Records*, includes a questionnaire that you can follow to gather information for your Business Impact Report.

IDENTIFYING CRITICAL SYSTEMS, APPLICATIONS AND VITAL RECORDS

Critical systems, applications and vital records are those you need to recover within one to three days for your business to survive. Although system management will dictate many data processing jobs, there should also be a list of processing job priorities that support the day-to-day operations for each department in your company.

One method of setting priorities would be to document all the functions performed by each department. A logical approach to this method would be to document routine activities over a period of several weeks. This documentation would then identify those critical applications and functions that are necessary to the department. Some of the key questions to consider are:

- If the online system was not available, how would your department continue to operate?

- What office equipment is used in your department, and could you operate for a period of five days without it?

- What is the minimum office space and staff you would need to continue essential operations?

- What forms are needed, if any, to perform data entry?

- What communications equipment would be necessary to continue operations?

- What employees are cross-trained to perform other key job functions?

Send the questionnaire to each department manager. <u>Worksheet 4</u> provides a sample questionnaire that you can customize and distribute.

When you receive the completed questionnaires, prepare a list of critical requirements and return to the department managers for priority rankings so they may be included in the Business Continuity Plan.

The priority rankings could be:

- **Critical Activities** — disruption of these exceeding one day would seriously impact the operation of the department.

- **Secondary Activities** — disruption of these exceeding one week would seriously impact the operation of the department.

- **Non-Critical Activities** — disruption of these would be an inconvenience, but would not seriously impact the operation of the department.

Worksheet 4

Business Continuity Plan — Sample Department Questionnaire

Objective: To determine what is critical for department operation, and develop measures to minimize loss in the event of a disaster.

This questionnaire is to aid in discussion between you and the Plan Coordinator.

NAME: _____   DATE: _____

TITLE: _____   NO. OF PERSONNEL: _____

DEPT/DIVISION: _____   LOCATION: _____

DEPT. FUNCTION: _____   PHONE: _____

Identifying critical functions

1.   Please identify the functions of your department or work group.

_____

_____

_____

_____

2.   What are the priority tasks, including manual functions, of your department? Please indicate if these tasks are performed daily, weekly, monthly, etc.

_____

_____

_____

_____

Attach additional pages as needed.

3.   List all resources required to perform your priority tasks. Include staff, preprinted forms, office equipment, computer equipment and telecommunication devices.

_____

_____

_____

_____

4.   Do you currently have procedures to replace critical equipment, forms and supplies in the event of a disaster? If no, please make replacement recommendations for each and the turn around time needed.

_____

_____

_____

_____

5.   What important reference materials or operating procedures are used in your department? How would these be replaced in a disaster?

_____

_____

_____

_____

6.   Should any departmental forms, supplies, equipment or reference manuals be stored in an off-site location? If yes, please identify.

_____

_____

_____

_____

Attach additional pages as needed.

7.   Identify the security and storage of original documents and vital records. How would this information be replaced in a disaster? Should any of these original documents be in a more protected place, e.g., off-site storage, company vault, etc.?

_____

_____

_____

_____

8.   What are your backup procedures for all stand-alone computer systems located within your department location? Do any of these critical backups need to be stored off-site?

_____

_____

_____

_____

9. Do you currently have a temporary operating procedure in place should a disaster occur? If yes, please summarize.

_____

_____

_____

_____

10. What other departments would be affected by a disruption in your daily business functions?

_____

_____

_____

_____

Attach additional pages as needed

11. How long can your department perform all of its business functions without the support of the data processing center? Assume that this loss of support occurred during your busiest or peak period? Check one only.

_____

_____

_____

_____

Attach additional pages for each service or software application.

Up to three days _____ Up to one-week _____ Up to one-month _____

Briefly describe the name and nature of the application/service provided by the data center.

_____

_____

_____

_____

12. Indicate a peak time of year, and/or a critical day of the week, if any, for this application.

_____

_____

Are there any other peak-load considerations?

_____

13. Have you developed any back-up procedures, which can be used to continue operations in the event that this software application is not available?

Yes _____   No _____

If yes, have the procedures been tested:

Within the last six months?   _____

In the past year?   _____

Over a year ago?   _____

Other   _____

14. What outside services or vendors do you rely on for normal operations?

_____

_____

_____

_____

15. Would a disaster in your department cause interruption to any reporting which is legally required?

_____

_____

16. Do you have current job descriptions available for your department?

_____

17. Identify personnel that are cross-trained for each position within your department

18. Who will be responsible for maintaining your piece of our company's Business Continuity Plan?

_____

19. Are there any other factors, which should be considered relating to planning for business continuity?

_____

_____

_____

_____

Attach additional pages as needed.

Estimate of Business Impact Due to Loss of Critical Software

The primary purpose of this section is to help the department manager estimate the impact of loss for those software applications identified in question #11. Use a separate worksheet for each software application.

Use the following codes for the next 3 questions to estimate loss potential.

(You may want to adjust these ranges to correspond to your company's size)

A = over $10,000,000

B = $1,000,000 to $10,000,000

C = $100,000 to $1,000,000

D = $10,000 to $100,000

E = up to $10,000

Software Application Name: _____

1.   Estimate lost revenue from fees, collections, interest penalties, etc., if this software application were not available for use.

        Day 1   _____

        Day 2   _____

        Day 4   _____

        1 Wk.   _____

        1 Mo.   _____

        Other   _____

2.   The loss of this application would negatively impact our customer base over time. The cost to the organization from lost business would be:

        Day 1:   _____

        Day 2 :   _____

        Day 4:   _____

        1 Week: _____

        1 Month: _____

        Other: _____

3.   The result of this application loss would be the following fines and penalties due to regulatory requirements: (Federal, state, and local)

Day 1:   _____

Day 2:   _____

Day 4:   _____

1 Week: _____

1 Month   _____

Other   _____

4.   The loss of this application would have legal ramifications due to regulatory statutes, contractual agreements, etc. Please specify.

_____

_____

_____

_____

5.   The loss of this application would keep your department from supplying services to outside customers. Please specify.

_____

_____

_____

_____

6.   Are there any other factors, which should be considered in evaluating the loss of this application?

_____

_____

_____

_____

7.   After thinking about your responses to the above questions, do you believe that this business process should be considered as "vital" to our company? If yes, indicate the appropriate choice below:

_____ Always

_____ During the following period of the year: _____

_____ During the following time of the month: _____

_____ During the following time of the week: _____

_____ Other time period (specify):   _____

USING YOUR BUSINESS IMPACT ANALYSIS

Identifying business loss exposure may seem difficult, but it can be relatively simple. Your two biggest problems may be getting started and maintaining objectivity. But once you have developed, distributed and conducted the department interviews, you have traveled a long way towards the completion of your continuity plan. So, let's begin analyzing the information you have gathered by answering the following questions:

What's your staying power?

First, consider what a "significant amount of money" is for your organization. At what dollar level is there only a slight concern, and therefore you would not want to invest time or money to protect against that loss? Ask senior management for their input on what they consider this number to be; a number of different answers should be expected.

Second, what is a "moderate amount of money?" For one company, this may be $10,000, for another, $10,000,000. At some level, a threshold will be identified where you would be concerned, and will want to consider protective measures against that loss.

Third, what is a "large amount of money?" This is the level where severe damage occurs. When this level is reached, a mandatory recovery plan should be considered and measures taken to reduce the risks associated with it.

While performing this analysis, do not forget the nonfinancial impacts of a disaster. The safety of staff, customer service, and regulatory or legal exposure can turn an insignificant amount of money into a large amount. Your company's business plan will also provide you with important information on areas requiring protection.

Timing your defense

Time should also be analyzed the same way as money. First, define what a short-term outage would be, which would not require any emergency action. Second, define a medium-term outage and determine what recovery action would be required. And third, define a long-term outage that would require the full implementation of your Business Continuity Plan.

What immediate resources do you need?

What are your minimal functional requirements? Analyze the information you gathered from the interviews, and determine what level of service must be provided to your customers. Then, determine what staff, records, equipment, facilities and systems are needed to provide that service. This will also help you to identify which resources are dispensable.

The effects of the outage may be tracked across related resources and dependent systems, identifying any cascading effects that may occur as a disrupted system affects other business functions may rely on.

When you begin the process of determining your business exposure and what areas of your business need protection, you will see that they will vary depending on whom you have interviewed. There are no absolute numbers, since your business is a changing entity. Loss estimates that were right two years ago or even yesterday may not be right today. Use your loss estimates to help you and the department manager prioritize applications and resources. Once this list of critical applications and resources has been determined, document them by using pre-formatted forms, which can be incorporated into your continuity plan. Examples of form content are in *Appendix C.*

The templates found in *Worksheet 5* can be used to list and graph outage costs for the first month. Once completed, they will help you determine the business functions/systems that are most critical to your business's day-to-day operations — you might be surprised how quickly your losses mount with time!

Develop Recovery Priorities

The outage impact/s and allowable outage times will enable you to develop and prioritize recovery strategies that the recovery team will implement during the plan's activation. For example, if your BIA determines that the business function must be recovered in four hours, you would need to take measures to meet that need. Similarly, if most applications could tolerate a 24-hour outage but a critical function could only be unavailable for eight hours, you would prioritize the necessary resources for the critical function. By prioritizing these recovery strategies, you can make more informed decisions regarding resource allocations and expenditures, saving time, effort and costs.

Identify Preventive Controls

The Business Impact Analysis can provide you with vital information about system availability and recovery requirements. In some cases, the outage impacts identified in the BIA may be mitigated or eliminated through preventive measures that deter, detect and/or reduce potential disasters. Whenever possible and cost-effective, preventive methods should be used rather than measures designed to recover the system after a disruption. A wide variety of preventive controls are available, depending on the type of system you have and the configuration. Examples of some common measures include:

- Appropriately sized, uninterruptible power supplies (UPS) to provide short-term backup power to all system components (including environmental and safety controls)

- Gasoline- or diesel-powered generators to provide long-term backup power

- Air conditioning systems with adequate excess capacity to permit failure of certain components, such as a compressor

- Fire suppression systems

- Fire and smoke detectors

- Water sensors in the computer room ceiling and floor

- Plastic tarps that can be unrolled over IT equipment to protect it from water damage

- Heat-resistant and waterproof containers for backup media and vital non-electronic records

- Emergency master system shutdown switches

- Offsite storage of backup media, non-electronic records, and system documentation

- Technical security controls such a cryptographic key management and least-privilege access controls

- Frequent, scheduled backups.

Document preventive controls in your Business Continuity Plan, and train personnel associated with the system on how and when to use them. Those controls must be maintained in good condition to ensure their effectiveness in an emergency.

Develop Technical Recovery Strategies

Recovery strategies provide a means for you to restore operations quickly and effectively following a disruption in service. The strategies should address the potential impacts identified in your BIA. Considerations for developing the strategy include cost, allowable outage time, security and integration with any larger organizational contingency plans.

Backup Methods

Critical applications and data should be backed up regularly. Policies should be simple to understand and should specify the frequency and types of backups (e.g., daily, weekly, incremental or full), based on the criticality and the frequency that new information is entered. Your backup policies should designate the location of the stored data, file naming conventions, tape rotation frequency and method for transporting data off-site. Data may be backed up on magnetic disk, tape or optical disks such as CD-ROMs. The specific method you choose for conducting backups should be based on system and data availability and integrity requirements. These methods include electronic vaulting, mirrored disks using direct access storage devices, and floppy disks.

Commercial data storage facilities are specially designed to archive media and protect data from threatening elements. If using off-site storage, data is backed up at the organization's facility and then labeled, packed, and transported to the storage facility. If the data is required for recovery or testing purposes, you can contact the facility and request specific data to be transported to your company or alternate facility. Commercial storage facilities often offer media transportation and response and recovery services.

When selecting an offsite storage facility, and vendor, consider the following:

- **Geographic area** – the distance from your company and the probability of the storage site being affected by the same disaster event as you company.

- **Accessibility** – the length of time necessary to retrieve the data from storage and the storages facility's operating hours.

- **Security** – the security capabilities of the storage facility and employee confidentiality, which must meet the data's sensitivity and security requirements.

- **Environment** – the structural and environmental conditions of the storage facility (i.e., temperature, humidity, fire prevention, and power management controls)

- **Cost** – the cost of shipping, operational fees and disaster response/recovery services.

While the traditional methods of backing up critical data have been considered cost-effective and practical for many purposes, there are vulnerabilities that became evident as a result of the September 11, 2001 terrorist attacks. Some firms — particularly smaller ones — sent records off-site only at daily or weekly intervals. As a result, when they lost their primary offices, they had to devote substantial resources to reconstruct records that had not yet been transferred to the backup facilities. The experience also suggested that recovering critical real-time processing operations from backup tapes is not generally realistic for large companies or critical, high-volume processing activities. Most larger companies now employ data "mirroring" or remote real-time transaction logging technologies through which transactions are transmitted immediately to a second (and in some cases, third) site. However, on September 11, in some cases where it appeared the appropriate protections were in place, problems such as out-of-date software, reduced system capacity, and inadequate telecommunications at the backup site were not discovered until operations were in the process of being recovered.

Alternate Site

Commercial recovery sites permit your company to continue computer, network and critical business operations in the event of a disaster. These sites and services are subscribed to by annual contract. When your company actually uses the site, other fees will be incurred in addition to the basic monthly charge.

Address site relocation for short-term, medium-term, and long-term disaster and disruption scenarios. Continuity planning for recovery facilities should consider location, size, capacity (computer and telecommunications) and required amenities necessary to recover the level of service required by the critical business functions. This includes planning for workspace, telephones, workstations, network connectivity, etc. Include logistical procedures for moving personnel to the recovery location, in addition to steps to obtain materials (media, documentation, supplies, etc.) from the off-site storage location. Also plans for lodging, meals and family considerations need to be addressed.

You may consider disruptions with long-term effects unlikely, but they should be accounted for in your Business Continuity Plan. Thus, your plan should include a strategy to recover and perform system operations at an alternate facility for an extended period. In general, three types of alternate sites are available:

- Dedicated site owned or operated by your company

- Reciprocal agreement with an internal or external organization

- Commercial recovery site.

Regardless of the type of alternate site you choose, the facility must be able to support system operations as defined in your BCP. The three alternate site types also may be categorized in terms of their operational readiness. Based on this factor, sites may be classified as cold sites, hot sites, mobile sites, and mirrored sites. Progressing from basic to advance, the sites are described below:

- **Cold Sites** typically consist of a facility with adequate space and infrastructure (electric power, telecommunications connections, and environmental controls) to support your IT system. The space may have raised floors and other attributes suited for IT operations. The site does not contain computer equipment and usually does not contain office automation equipment, such as telephones, fax machines, or copiers. Your company is normally responsible for providing and installing necessary equipment and telecommunications capabilities.

- **Warm Sites** are partially equipped office spaces that contain some or all of the system hardware, software, telecommunications, and power sources. The warm site is maintained in an operational status ready to receive your system. The site may need to be prepared before receiving your system and recovery personnel. In many cases, a warm site may serve as a normal operational facility for another system or function, and in the event you activate your Business Continuity Plan, the normal activities are displaced temporarily to accommodate you.

- **Hot Sites** are office and computer spaces appropriately sized to support your system requirements and configured with the necessary hardware, supporting infrastructure and support personnel. A hot site has all the equipment needed for the enterprise to continue operation, including office space and furniture, telephone jacks, and computer equipment. Subscriptions to commercial hot sites are based on hardware specifications required to recover a "like" computer configuration.

- **Mobile Sites** are self-contained, transportable shells, custom-fitted with specific telecommunications and computer equipment necessary to meet your system requirements. They are available for lease through commercial vendors. The facility often is contained in a tractor-trailer and may be driven to and set up at a location you choose. In most cases, to be a viable recovery solution, design the mobile site in advance with the vendor and sign a service level agreement between the two of you. This is necessary because the time required to configure the mobile site can be extensive, and without prior coordination, the time to deliver the mobile site may exceed your allowable outage time. In addition, local building permits, building codes and zoning regulations will need to be addressed, even if the mobile site is temporary.

- **Mirrored Sites** are fully redundant facilities with full, real-time information mirroring. Mirrored sites are identical to your primary site in all technical respects. These sites provide the highest degree of availability because the data is processed and stored at the primary and alternate site simultaneously. These sites typically are designed, built, operated and maintained by you.

There are obvious cost and ready-time differences among the five options. The mirrored site is the most expensive choice, but it comes closest to virtually 100 percent availability, if it is geographically outside the disaster zone. Cold sites are the least expensive to maintain; however, they require substantial time to acquire and install necessary equipment. Partially equipped sites such as warm sites fall in the middle of the spectrum. In many cases, mobile sites are delivered to the desired location within 24-48 hours. However, installation time can increase this response time, and, if the mobile resources are in use by another customer, they may not be available. *Figure 1* summarizes the criteria that can be employed to determine which type of alternate site meets your organization's requirements. Moreover, analyze sites further based on the specific requirements defined in your BIA. As sites are evaluated, be sure that the system's security, management, operational and technical controls, such as firewalls and physical access controls, are compatible with the prospective site.

Figure 1 – Alternate Site Criteria Selection

Site	Cost	Hardware Equipment	Telecommunications	Setup Time	Location
Cold Site	Low	None	None	Long	Fixed
Warm Site	Medium	Partial	Partial/Full	Medium	Fixed
Hot Site	Medium/High	Full	Full	Short	Fixed
Mobile Site	High	Dependent	Dependent	Dependent	Not Fixed
Mirrored Site	High	Full	Full	None	Fixed

These alternate sites may be owned and operated by you (internal recovery) or may be contracted for commercially. If contracting with a commercial vendor, adequate testing time, workspace, security requirements, hardware requirements, telecommunications requirements, support services, and recovery days (how long you can occupy the space during recovery period) must be negotiated and clearly stated in the contract. Be aware that multiple customers may contract with the vendor for the same alternate site; as a result, the site may be unable to accommodate all of the customers if a disaster affects enough of those customers at the same time. The vendor's policy on how this situation is addressed and how priority status is determined should be negotiated. In addition, consider the availability of multiple vendor facilities in different locations.

Two or more companies with similar or identical IT configurations and backup technologies may enter a formal agreement to serve as alternate sites for each other or to enter a joint contract for an alternate site. This type of site is setup via a reciprocal agreement or memorandum of understanding (MOU). Enter into a reciprocal agreement carefully because each site must be able to support the other, in addition to its own workload, in the event of a disaster. This type of agreement requires the recovery sequence for the applications from both companies to be prioritized from a joint perspective. Conduct a test at the partnering sites to evaluate the extra processing thresholds, compatible system and backup configurations, sufficient telecommunications connections, and compatible security measures. In general, reciprocal agreements are seldom effective or reliable.

Equipment Replacement

If your system is damaged or destroyed or if your primary site is unavailable, necessary hardware and software will need to be activated or procured quickly and delivered to the alternate location. Three basic strategies exist to prepare for equipment replacement. When selecting the most appropriate strategy, do not assume that transportation systems such as airlines, railroads, road access or subways will be operating or that your equipment vendors will be able to respond.

- **Vendor Agreements** — As your Business Continuity Plan is being developed, service level agreements (SLAs) with hardware, software and support vendors can be made for emergency maintenance service. Include alternate vendors in this process in the event your primary vendor is unavailable or unable to respond. The SLA should specify the vendor's response time after being notified. The agreement also should give your company priority status for the shipment of replacement equipment over equipment being purchased for normal operations. SLAs should also discuss the priority status your company will receive in the event of a catastrophic disaster involving multiple vendor clients. In such cases, organizations with health- and safety-dependent processes will often receive the highest priority for shipment. The details of these negotiations should be documented in the SLA, which should be maintained with the continuity plan.

- **Equipment Inventory** — Required equipment may be purchased in advance and stored at a secure offsite location, such as an alternate site where recovery operations will take place or at another location where they will be stored and then shipped to the alternate site. However, this solution has certain drawbacks. An organization must commit financial resources to purchase this equipment in advance, and the equipment could become obsolete or unsuitable for use over time because system technologies and requirements change.

- **Existing Compatible Equipment** — Equipment currently housed and used by the contracted hot site or by another organization within your company may be used. Agreements made with hot sites and reciprocal internal sites stipulate that similar equipment will be available for contingency use by your organization.

When evaluating the choices, you should consider that purchasing equipment when needed is cost-effective, but can add significant overhead time to recovery while waiting for shipment and setup; storing unused equipment is costly but allows recovery operations to begin more quickly. Based on impacts discovered through your BIA, consider the possibility of a widespread disaster such as the September, 11, 2001 attacks, requiring mass equipment replacement and transportation delays that would extend the recovery period. Regardless of the strategy selected, keep a list of equipment needs and specifications with the Business Continuity Plan.

Cost Considerations

- Ensure that the strategy chosen can be implemented effectively with available personnel and financial resources.

- The cost of each type of alternate site, equipment replacement and storage option under consideration should be weighed against budget limitations.

- Determine contingency planning expenses, such as alternate site contract fees, and those that are less obvious, such as the cost of implementing company-wide business continuity program awareness and contractor support.

- The budget must be sufficient to encompass software, hardware, travel, shipping, testing, plan-training programs, awareness programs, labor hours, other contracted services, and any other applicable resources (e.g., desks, telephones, fax machines, pens, and paper).

- Perform a cost-benefit analysis to identify the optimum recovery strategy. *Figure 2* provides a template for evaluating cost considerations.

Figure 2 – Recovery Strategy Budget Planning Template

		Vendor Costs	Hardware Costs	Software Costs	Travel/ Shipping Costs	Labor/ Contractor Costs	Testing Costs	Supply Costs
Alternate Site	Cold Site							
	Warm Site							
	Hot Site							
	Mobile Site							
	Mirrored Site							
Off-Site Storage	Commercial							
	Internal							
Equipment Replacement	SLAs							
	Storage							
	Existing Use							

Vendor Supplied Equipment

Some vendors will confirm in writing or verbally "should your company experience a disaster, you will receive the next comparable system from the manufacturing line for shipment to the recovery site." There are risks associated with this means of recovery, such as obtaining peripheral equipment, shipping delays and preparing the equipment for operation.

Other services to consider are:

- Off-site storage location (for both the primary and alternate sites)

- Cleaning and restoration companies

- Software vendors

- Temporary personnel providers

- Office supply vendors

- Networking and telephone providers

- Service bureaus

- Transportation and lodging

- Car rental agencies

- Couriers

- Banks

- Fire, police, hospitals, ambulance service

- Civil Defense

- Red Cross

- Post Office

- Regulatory agencies

- Power and utility companies

- Newspapers, radio and TV stations

- Contractors

- Real Estate Agencies

- Law Firms

Having compiled the list of vendors you will need to contact after a disaster, enter the vendor information on the *Vendor Call List*; see *Worksheet 5*. Document any vendor-specific notification procedures in front of the Vendor Call List, or reference where they can be found within your plan. It is helpful to organize the Vendor Call List by common services or products, for example, computer hardware and office equipment suppliers, stationery providers, consultants, etc. Identify only those vendors needed during the recovery process and in the order they should be contacted. A sample vendor letter to request information regarding emergency procedures is provided in *Figure 3*.

Supporting Personnel

The Business Continuity Plan must not focus entirely on IT requirements. Your company's personnel are an essential element because there is no point in recovering a business system that cannot be used.

Figure 3 – Sample Vendor Letter

Date _____

Vendor name   _____

Address   _____

Dear   _____,

(*Company Name*) is a user of your product/service.

We are currently in the process of developing a Business Continuity Plan. Should we experience a fire or other disaster at (*give address(es)*), we may need to perform our operations at another site and need expedited shipments.

Please advise us what special arrangements need to be implemented with your company so that we may incorporate these procedures into our plan.

If you require amendments to our existing contract, please prepare them for our signature.

Sincerely,

Name

Title

Phone

Worksheet 5 – Sample Vendor Call Sheet

Vendor Name/Address   **Contact**   **Type of Service/Product**

_____   _____   _____

_____   _____   Phone _____

_____   Emergency Phone   _____

E-mail _____   _____

Notes _____

Vendor Name/Address   **Contact**   **Type of Service/Product**

_____   _____   _____

_____   _____   Phone _____

_____   Emergency Phone   _____

E-mail _____   _____

Notes _____

Vendor Name/Address   **Contact**   **Type of Service/Product**

_____   _____   _____

_____   _____   Phone _____

_____   Emergency Phone   _____

E-mail _____   _____

Notes _____

> *Note: It is helpful to organize the Vendor Call List by common services or products, for example, computer hardware and office equipment suppliers, stationary providers, consultants, etc. Identify only those vendors needed during the recovery process and the order they should be contacted.*

Worksheet 6 – Cumulative Outage Costs

Instructions: Enter the dollar total from Part II of the Business Impact Questionnaire for each application. Total each column and then graph totals on the "Loss Curve in Millions" graph located on the next page.

Depart-ment	Description of Application	Day 1	Day 2	Day 4	1 Week	1 Month
	Totals:					

Loss Curve in Millions

$ Amount					
Length of Outage:	1 day	2 days	4 days	1 week	1 month

STEP 6 — SELECTING YOUR RECOVERY TEAMS

Roles and Responsibilities

Having selected and implemented your system recovery strategy, you should designate appropriate teams to implement the strategy. Each team should be trained and ready to go in the event of a disruptive situation requiring plan activation. Assign recovery personnel to one of the several specific teams that will respond to the event, recover capabilities and return the critical systems to normal operations. To do so, they will need to understand their team's goal in the recovery effort, the steps they are to execute and how their team relates to other teams.

The list that follows is not definitive so construct your teams to best suit the needs of your company. For smaller companies, you may want to combine a number of tasks to a smaller number of teams, or even to one team, as appropriate.

Assign a team leader to each team and enough members, as well as backups for essential team members, to ensure that the team's responsibilities can be met. The following teams reflect the tasks at hand:

- **Administration**: This team reports to the command center to support the emergency management team and the business recovery coordinators; provides administrative support services, including travel and lodging, petty cash disbursement, notifications to customers, and preparation of all reports for the recovery operation.

- **Business Function Recovery**: This team responds to and manages any serious interruption to specific business function operations; develops recovery strategies and procedures based on a business impact analysis.

- **Command Center**: The command center team activates the facility used for assembly of the emergency management team, help desk team, administration team, and the business recovery coordinators, when a disaster has occurred. They are also responsible for the initial distribution of supplies, forms and off-site boxes stored at the warehouse. The warehouse and facilities personnel make up this team.

- **Damage Assessment**: This recovery team assesses the damage of the disabled facility and its contents, both preliminary (immediately after an event) and comprehensive assessments. Activities are coordinated with the business recovery coordinator, IT recovery coordinator, emergency management and facility preparation team. Members of this team include building engineers, data services and risk management personnel, and any related vendors or technical experts.

> *Note: Hazardous materials teams are allowed in facilities first when hazardous materials are involved. Damage assessment teams must wait until access has been granted to the damaged facility.*

- **Emergency Management**: The emergency management team provides overall management to all recovery teams; authorization for disaster declaration; business recovery functions for all operating business units; guidance for all restoration activities; company expenditure arrangements and public relations information.

- **Emergency Purchasing**: This team coordinates the replacement (purchase and/or lease) of all damaged equipment at the disabled facility, as well as equipment required for alternate operations. They also coordinate the delivery and installation of such equipment at the alternate site. This team handles the procurements for all information resources, general office needs and facilities requirements. This team may also request a suspension of purchasing rules and regulations to facilitate recovery.

- **Equipment Installation**: This team controls the installation of all terminals, PCs and printers at the alternate site. Personnel for this team are primarily from PC/LAN and telecommunications support areas. This team interfaces with all business units and works directly with the emergency purchasing and facilities preparation teams.

- **Executive Management**: The Company's executive management communicates support of the business recovery process by issuing a formal policy statement; periodically reviewing the recovery assumptions, potential loss assumptions, strategic considerations and definitions of resumption priorities. Executive management ensures that adequate resources are devoted to the project by approving recovery strategies, possible alternatives, funding and ongoing maintenance.

- **Facilities Preparation**: The facilities preparation team coordinates and directs all activities necessary to restore, build and/or lease a replacement building. The team reviews business unit requests for office space; provides alternate site facilities to continue critical business functions; and participates in damage assessment.

- **Finance**: The finance group oversees proper authorization and support of expenses during emergency procurement.

- **Information Technology**: The IT team maps the recovery of the information resources (mainframe computer and associated service, telecommunications and connectivity, LANs, WANs, and PCs) for business function recovery at an alternate site. The organization may have a central computing center and/or distributed systems, which would dictate the size, complexity and areas of responsibility of the teams. The basic responsibilities include the following:

  - *Applications* — restore and support application systems at the recovery center and define data file retention periods for off-site storage.

  - *Data Base Administration* — restores all critical data bases and evaluates their integrity; closely coordinates file synchronization and balancing conditions with the applications team prior to resuming production processing.

  - *Data Security* — maintains data security of the electronic records and files throughout the recovery operations. Data security includes passwords, assigned access levels, security software (audit trails, firewalls), encryption, data backups, and security levels for records (confidential, personal, or open).

- *IT Recovery Coordinator* — coordinates all activities of the recovery teams for the company's central computing center and works closely with the business recovery coordinator and the other teams. Depending on the size of the company or the organization, this function may also be performed by the business recovery coordinator.

- *Help Desk* — processes all end-user inquiries and requests concerning the recovered computer systems during the recovery effort.

- *Mainframe Distribution* — controls all printed output. This team controls output created by outside vendors. This team interfaces with all business recovery teams and the operations team.

- *Networks* — restore both voice and data-critical circuits and maintain a backup telecommunications network. The team interfaces closely with the business recovery, systems software, operations and facility preparation teams.

- *Operations* — support restoration of the mainframe utilities, critical applications and databases, I/O controls, and schedule all production applications. Most team members are staff from central computer operations.

- *Off-Site Storage* — retrieves all required electronic media from the off-site storage location and transports it to the recovery center. Reestablishes or maintains alternate off-site storage locations for rotations of electronic vital records throughout the recovery effort.

- *System Software* — restores the operation system and all subsystems at the alternate recovery center. The team also prepares the operating system configuration to be used in the alternate site and restored primary home site.

- **Legal**: The legal team insures that legal issues or procedures related to potential company liabilities are addressed in the plan.

- **Physical Security**: This recovery team provides physical security for all personnel, the buildings and all alternate sites.

- **Public Relations**: The public relations team provides accurate, essential and timely information to employees, employees' families, the media and customers about what has happened and how the recovery plan is working. This team ensures the appropriate spokesperson addresses environmental, health and safety issues.

Team Leaders

A team leader is assigned from each business unit to be responsible for coordinating all team planning, testing and recovery activities. Ideally, team leaders are members of first-line management or project leaders with strong leadership and organization skills, and are detail-oriented with a basic knowledge of the business unit's functions. They are responsible for all liaison activities between the company's recovery coordinators and other team leaders.

Team Members

The skills and abilities of the combined team members must cover a wide range of responsibilities, many of which are dictated by the business function(s). Ideally, team members are supervisors who can effectively invoke a business unit's recovery process in the event of a disaster. Team members are responsible for researching their respective parts of the plan and for meeting deadlines.

Refer to *Figure 4* as a guideline to establish your recovery teams and associated responsibilities. The blank form in *Worksheet 7* can be used as a guideline for establishing your *Emergency Call Sheet* that includes member names, contact numbers, e-mail and areas of responsibility.

> *Note: The specific types of teams needed are based on the system affected. The size of each team, the title given the team, and the hierarchy of each will depend upon the specific nature of your company.*

Choose personnel to staff these teams based on their skills and knowledge. Ideally, staff the teams with the personnel responsible for the same or similar operation under normal condition. For example, for your client and web servers, your Server Recovery Team members should include the server administrators. Team members must understand not only the contingency plan purpose, but also the procedures necessary for executing the recovery strategy. Teams need to be sufficient in size to remain viable if some members are unavailable to respond, or designate alternate team members. Similarly, team members need to be familiar with the goals and procedures of other teams to facilitate inter-team coordination.

Once the team membership is established, train the team leaders, members and alternates in their responsibilities. Include the following in your training program.

*   Team responsibilities;

*   Team membership;

*   The emergency action plans (see Step 7); and,

*   Other relevant sections of the Business Continuity Plan.

Figure 4

A Guideline for Recovery Team Identification

and Areas of Responsibility

The Emergency Response Team

The purpose and responsibility of the Emergency Response Team is to coordinate all activities during the recovery period. The general areas of responsibility may include implementing administrative controls and communicating the recovery status to senior management.

Sample Responsibilities:

- Disaster declaration

- Coordination of recovery activities

- Documentation of recovery activities

- Senior management liaison

- Plan execution

- Staff assignments

- Activation of recovery teams

- Communication with system users

- Financial and policy decisions

- Vendor interface

The Emergency Reconstruction Team

The purpose and responsibility of the Emergency Reconstruction Team is to restore the primary facility back to full operation.

Sample Responsibilities:

- Damage assessment

- Security

- Equipment salvage

- Equipment installation

- Site planning

- Site construction

- Vendor interface

- Restoration of primary site

The Off-Site Recovery Operations Team 1

The purpose and responsibility of the Off-Site Recovery Team 1 is to establish operations at the alternate computer site and prepare it for workload processing.

Sample Responsibilities:

- Security

- Establish command center at recovery site or other pre-planned location

- Relocation of equipment, personnel and supplies

- Obtain system and other documentation

- Prepare recovery site and command center for operation

- Establish telecommunications network

- Coordinate transportation of people and supplies

The Off-Site Recovery Operations Team 2

The purpose and responsibility of Off-Site Recovery Operations Team 2 is to provide processing of critical software applications at the alternate computer facility.

Sample Responsibilities:

- Workload scheduling

- System operations

- Systems software, Server, LAN/WAN, Database, Network, Applications and Telecommunications Recovery

Backup Staff Team

The purpose and responsibility of the Backup Staff Team is to remain available for future team assignments. Members of this team would include computer staff and other key personnel not assigned to a recovery team.

Worksheet 7

Sample Emergency Response Team Assignments & Call Sheet

The Emergency Response Team   Page _____ of _____

Team Leader   Name: _____

Address: _____

City _____ State _____ Zip _____

Home: _____ Work: _____ Cell: _____

Pager: _____ E-Mail: _____

To be contacted by: _____

Backup Team Leader   Name: _____

Address: _____

City _____ State _____ Zip _____

Home: _____ Work: _____ Cell: _____

Pager: _____ E-Mail: _____

To be contacted by: _____

Team Member   Name: _____

Address: _____

City _____ State _____ Zip _____

Home: _____ Work: _____ Cell: _____

Pager: _____ E-Mail: _____

To be contacted by: _____

Area of Responsibility: _____

Emergency Response Team Assignments & Call Sheet

The Emergency Response Team   Page _____ of _____

Team Member   Name: _____

Address: _____

City _____ State _____ Zip _____

Home: _____ Work: _____ Cell: _____

Pager: _____ E-Mail: _____

To be contacted by: _____

Area of responsibility: _____

Team Member   Name: _____

Address: _____

City _____ State _____ Zip _____

Home: _____ Work: _____ Cell: _____

Pager: _____ E-Mail: _____

To be contacted by: _____

Area of responsibility: _____

Team Member   Name: _____

Address: _____

City _____ State _____ Zip _____

Home: _____ Work: _____ Cell: _____

Pager: _____ E-Mail: _____

To be contacted by: _____

Area of responsibility: _____

STEP 7 — DEVELOPING YOUR RECOVERY STRATEGIES AND ACTION PLANS

This section addresses recovery strategies and the emergency action plans that recovery teams implement. These plans are geared to protect the critical business functions that you determined by performing the Business Impact Analysis.

The action plans you develop describe in detail the procedures to recover each business function affected by the disruption. Write the action plans in such a way that various groups of personnel could understand the instructions and implement them in a timely manner. The plans should be flexible to respond to changing internal and external conditions and new threat scenarios. The action plans will be more effective if written to address specific types of scenarios such as:

- Critical personnel are not available;

- Critical buildings or facilities have been destroyed, or geographic regions are not accessible;

- Equipment malfunctions (hardware, telecommunications, operational equipment);

- Software and data are not accessible or are corrupted;

- Utilities are not available (power, telecommunications); and

- Critical documentation and/or records are not available.

In order to facilitate a recovery regardless of the type or duration of a disaster, you can implement multiple recovery strategies categorized into three levels. Each level is designed to provide an effective recovery solution equally matched to the duration of the emergency condition. You should determine the appropriate time scales for each level.

- **Level 1: Short-Term Outage** *(Less than 48 Hours– Ride-it-Out)*

  A short-term outage is defined as the period of time your company does not require computerized operations, or where the length of the outage would not allow adequate time to restore and begin using automated equipment.

- **Level 2: Medium-Term Outage** *(48 Hours to 6 Weeks)*

  A medium-term outage is defined as the period of time your company will execute its formal disaster recovery strategy, which includes actually declaring a disaster. A disaster may either be declared company wide or only for the effected department or building. The decision to declare a disaster will be based on the amount of time and expense that is required to implement the formal recovery and the anticipated impact to your company's bottom line.

- **Level 3: Long-Term Outage** *(6 Weeks or More – Relocation)*

    A long-term outage would be defined as the period of time that your company would exceed the allowed occupancy time at an alternate site or other primary recovery strategy. This phase of recovery may initiate a permanent physical move of your company's personnel and resources.

Recovery Strategy Overview

A general strategy for recovery is shown in *Figure 6*, below, and would be implemented once the Emergency Response Team Leader determines that a declaration of disaster is required.

Figure 6 – Sample Recovery Strategy Overview

Steps	Instruction
1. Evacuate affected facility	If the emergency requires an evacuation of employees, execute evacuation plans contained in the Emergency Procedures section. (Appendices)
2. Go to staging area.	Follow building evacuation instructions.
3. Determine length of outage.	Review written and verbal damage assessment reports from facilities and civil authorities and then estimate the amount of time the facility will be unavailable.
4. Select disaster level.	Based on the estimated duration of the outage, declare the disaster event as a L1 (less than 48 hrs.), L2 (48 hrs. to 6 weeks) or L3 (6 weeks or longer).
5. Activate alternate facilities.	Contact alternate facilities identified in the Facilities sections. Confirm their availability and alert them of our estimated time of arrival.

Steps	Instruction
6. Release personnel from the staging area.	Once the disaster level has been selected, release all personnel from the staging area to their assigned recovery location: • Non-essential personnel – Home • Recovery Site Team – Alternate Facility • End Users – Alternate Facility • End Users – Alternate Facility • Command Center Staff – Alternate Facility • Crisis Management Team – Alternate Facility
7. Command Center is established by the Recovery Site Team (RST)	RST personnel are the first to arrive at the alternate site to setup and organize the command center prior to the arrival of the Crisis Management Team (CMT) and support personnel. The following representatives are required at the Command Center within 1-3 hours. • Crisis Management Team • Emergency Response Team Lead • Business Restoration Team Lead • Recovery Site Team Lead
8. Establish situation desk.	At the command center, establish a dedicated line with operator to field all incoming calls. Announce command phone number to all recovery participants.
9. Review recovery priorities.	Review the critical business functions on a department-by-department basis to determine who is most affected by the disaster. Group departments by recovery resource requirements, time frames and co-location requirements.
10. Create technology-shopping list.	Once the technology requirements of the affected department(s) are known, create a requirements list for the IT support staff.
11. Contact quick ship vendors.	Using vendor contacts (quick-ship) or local sources located in the LAN Restoration section of the BCP, order replacement technology indicated on the requirements list.
12. Retrieve electronic/hard copy vital records.	Retrieve vital records from the off-site storage location. Have records shipped and staged at the alternate site.

Steps	Instruction
13. Setup replacement Local Area Network	Restore priority Server to support critical business function.
14. Activate short-term recovery strategies.	Instruct each department to initiate their short-term recovery strategies. These strategies will be used while the replacement LAN/WAN circuits are implemented.
15. Populate alternate facility.	Once the replacement LAN/WAN is functional, notify the Business Restoration/Resumption Team that departments can now begin executing their L2 recovery strategies.

Once the alternate site has been secured, the Recovery Site Team will configure the command center and recovery space. *Figure 7* provides a sample configuration for general work areas and the command center:

Figure 7 — Sample Configuration of Work Areas

Recovery Area	Configuration
Command Center	• Occupancy 15 • Room – private, 750 sq. ft. • Conference table • Phones – 5 • Fax – 15 • Office Equipment – copier, typewriter, PC, Printer, folding tables • Office Supplies – flip charts, stationary, writing supplies • Communications – Walkie-talkies, tape recorder, cellular phones.

Recovery Area	Configuration
Work Area Recovery	• Occupancy – 50 • Room – 5,000 sq. ft. • Folding Tables – each workstation needs to be 3 ft. apart • Phones – 50 • Fax – 3 • Office Equipment – copier, typewriter, tape recorder, 15 pre-configured laptops • Office Supplies – flip charts, stationary, writing supplies • Communications – 3 fax lines, 10 modems, 50 voice lines
Mail Room	Occupancy – 2 Room – 250 sq. ft. Phone – 1 • Office Equipment – scale, postage meter • Supplies – Mailing/shipping supplies
Vital Records Staging	• Occupancy – 2 • Room – private, 300 sq. ft. • Office Equipment – folding tables, metal racks

In *Figure 8*, you will find a detailed sample Action Plan that addresses a worst-case scenario of a computer facility that has experienced severe damage. It is based on the use of an alternate processing site and contains information necessary to decide the level of disaster, whether to notify the recovery teams and whether the notification process for the recovery site management and vendors should be implemented. It will also provide guidelines for site reconstruction, and moving operations to the alternate processing site.

In *Figure 9*, you will find a sample Action Plan that addresses the procedures a payroll department might use to aid in the hiring, separation and payment of employees if automated systems are not available.

Figure 8 – Sample Action Plan - Data Center

Background Information

The action plan that follows provides the activities of the recovery teams during the recovery process. It contains the information needed to determine if a disaster has occurred and to decide whether to activate the recovery teams. Information about the hot site, notification procedures, processing at the recovery site, guidelines for reconstructing the primary site and returning to the restored site are provided.

This Action Plan is in the form of a list. The required activities are in the order in which they should be accomplished and by whom.

Sample Action Plan Task List

Scenario: Total Destruction of the Data Center

Stage 1 – Disaster Event

Step		Responsibility
001	**Is this a life-threatening situation?**	*Mgr. on duty*
	If yes, go to step 002; if not, go directly to 004	
002	**Evacuate area and notify the Emergency Response Team.**	*Mgr. on duty*
	002a. Begin to evacuate the building as defined in the Human Resources and Building Safety Manual.	
	002b. Notify the Emergency Response Team, informing them of the emergency situation.	
003	**Handle medical emergencies.**	*Mgr. on duty*
	003a. Administer first aid if possible, and if personnel are properly trained.	
	003b. If after normal business hours, call 911 for emergency assistance.	
	003c. If during normal business hours, contact the Company Medical Office at extension xxxx	
004	**Determine if there is property damage.**	*Standard Operations*
	If yes, notify the appropriate civil authorities; police (ph#:_____); fire (ph#:_____); Security Personnel (ph#:_____).	

If not, go directly to step 007a.

005   Shut down the equipment. (Emergency Mode)   *Standard Operations*

005a. If an orderly shut down is not feasible, break glass
above emergency power disconnect, switch off the main
circuit breaker on the electrical panel outside the computer
room and follow the procedures in Step 002.

005b. If an orderly shut down is feasible, switch off the main
circuit breaker on the electrical panel outside the computer
room and follow the procedures described in Step 002.

006   Protect the equipment by following the   *Standard Operations*

equipment protection procedure in the IS Operations Manual.

Stage 2

007   Activation of the Emergency Response Team   *Standard Operations*

007a. Notify the Emergency Response Team Leader.

007b. If the Recovery Coordinator, or the backup cannot be
found, the first person contacted should assume their
responsibilities and complete 007c through 007i.

007c. Contact members of the Emergency Response Team.

007d. Designate other members as required, if assigned members
are not available.

007e. Advise the team members of the potential disaster situation.

007f. Advise team members to meet at an appropriate location,
close to the facility, but out of danger and restricted areas.

007g. Notify the leaders of the Recovery Operations and Emergency
Rebuilding Teams.

007h. Advise the Emergency Rebuilding Team leader of the potential

disaster situation, and instruct the leader to have his team

meet the Emergency Response Team at the designated location

to assess the situation.

007i. Notify the Recovery Operations Team leader that their team

should be activated. Ask them to obtain a copy of the Business

Continuity Plan.

008 Notify Vendors. *Emergency Response Leader*

008a. Decide which vendors are to be contacted for

assessing the data center's ability to function.

008b. Contact and assemble the appropriate vendors.

009 Assess status of the primary site; estimate *Emergency Rebuilding Leader*

recovery time.

009a. Obtain approval to enter the site to assess damages.

009b. Assemble the Emergency Response Team and the

appropriate vendors notified in Step 008b.

009c. Conduct a detailed assessment of the site's condition,

support services, equipment, and available supplies.

009d. Identify the equipment that has been damaged.

009e. Identify physical damages to the site's environment.

009f. Identify usable equipment, files, and supplies.

009g. Create a list of all property that must be replaced or repaired.

009h. Confer with vendors and determine the minimum and maximum

estimated times to recover the data center.

010 Determine the action required (confer with the *Emergency Response Leader*

Emergency Rebuilding Team Leader) based on the maximum

estimated time determined in step 009, and if it exceeds the

maximum time to resume service, consider declaring a disaster.

011   **Determine if the recovery site will be needed.** If   *Emergency Response Leader*

yes, go to Step 012. If not, go directly to *Stage 4, Reconstruction of the*

Primary Site.

012   **Declare a disaster.**   Emergency Response Leader

012a. Notify senior management and user management of the

intent to declare a disaster.

012b. Activate the notification procedures with the Recovery Center.

012c. Notify the leader of the Recovery Operations Team of

the intent to declare a disaster.

012d. Notify the off-site storage facility to implement emergency

procedures.

012e. Notify appropriate insurance companies.

012f. Notify the appropriate vendors that additional equipment

will be needed at the recovery site.

013   **Remain available for team assignments**.   *Recovery Operations Teams 1 & 2*

014   **Activate Recovery Operations Team.**   *Emergency Response Leader*

015   **Establish Emergency Command Center.**   *Emergency Response Leader*

016   **Notify support vendors of the intention to**   *Emergency Response Leader*

operate at the recovery site.

016a. Notify equipment and software vendors of the operating status.

016b. Notify supply vendors to restore stock levels.

016c. Arrange for the shipment of supplies from the damage site

to the recovery center.

017   **Notify vendors of move to the Recovery**   *Emergency Response Leader*

Center.

018   **Go to the Recovery Center**.   *Recovery Operations Teams*

018a. Arrange for transportation to the Recovery Center and

lodging, if necessary. Confer with Recovery Operations Team Leader.

018b   Deliver files and manuals from off-site storage.

018c. Follow security procedures for entry to the Recovery Center.

018d. Follow vendor procedures for establishing the command center at the Recovery Center, or other pre-planned location. Notify the Emergency Response Team of the command center phone number(s).

018e. Establish a schedule for steps 019, 020, 021, 022, 023.

018f. Notify the Emergency Response Team of the schedule for completing steps 019 through 023.

018g. Coordinate obtaining salvaged files from the Emergency Rebuilding Team.

019   Restore telecommunications and operating   *Recovery Operations Teams*
software.

019a. Secure the operating system at the Recovery Center.

019b. Restore the communications network

019c. Run the installation verification to test equipment validity, software, operating procedures, telecommunications and local terminals.

019d. Restore and rebuild program libraries.

019e. Restore software applications.

019f. Restore and rebuild catalogs.

019g. Rebuild database and systems.

019h. Update the Emergency Response Team of the recovery status.

019i. Verify all major subsystems.

019j. Run a test job to determine the completeness of the backup configuration.

019k. Notify the Emergency Response Team of the configuration status.

019l. Remain at the Recovery Center to assist with production.

020   **Establish a production schedule at the**   *Recovery Operations Teams*

Recovery Center.

020a. Document the recovery operating production schedule.

020b. Verify the availability of data, documentation, supplies and staff.

021   **Recover production jobs.**   *Recovery Operations Teams*

021a. Restore production files in accordance with the

schedule developed in step 020.

021b. Return all files used in restoration, to the off-site storage facility.

022   **Restore production systems with current data.**   *Recovery Operations Teams*

022a. Run necessary file updates.

022b. Back-up all recovered and updated files. Store off-site.

022c. Notify the Emergency Response Team of the

status of vital records.

023   **Establish telecommunications network**.   *Recovery Operations Teams*

023a. Test software applications with each user area.

024b. Notify the Emergency Response Team that programs

are available to end-users.

Stage 3

024   **Monitor the progress of the recovery effort.**   *Emergency Response Team*

024a. Establish Recovery Log.

024b. Establish a schedule for receiving progress reports

from the Recovery Operations teams at the Recovery Center.

025   **Obtain additional equipment if needed.**   *Recovery Team Designee*

025a. Contact vendors providing the additional equipment

and agree on an acceptable delivery schedule.

025b. Contact vendors providing the additional communications

equipment and agree on an acceptable delivery schedule.

025c. Inform the Emergency Response Team and the

Recovery Operations Team members of the delivery schedules.

025d. Advise the Recovery Center Manager of the

established delivery schedules.

026   Obtain necessary supplies.   *Recovery Team Designee*

026a. Contact vendors and establish an acceptable

delivery time for supplies.

026b. Advise the Recovery Operations Team of the schedule.

026c. Advise the Recovery Center Manager of the

delivery schedule.

027   Implement emergency control procedures.   *Emergency Response Team*

027a. Call an emergency meeting of the IS Management Team.

027b. Conduct a briefing on the situation, anticipated

recovery time, recovery process/action items,

and notification schedules (internal and external).

027c. Obtain agreement on the application priorities,

notification schedules and distribution of available

equipment. (e.g., printers, terminals, etc.)

027d Establish communication procedure for setting up

meetings as necessary.

028   Coordinate the recovery process.   *Emergency Response Team*

029   Establish communications update procedures with users.

Senior Management

029a. Review the progress of the primary site restoration

and the schedule to resume operations at the alternate site(s).

029b. Establish a schedule for providing management and end users

with progress reports.

030   Commence Recovery Center operations.   *Recovery Operations Teams*

030a. Operate under normal operating schedules using the

recovery priority list.

030b. Continue normal off-site storage procedures.

030c. Log any timing issues and operating problems for

each recovery job.

031   Provide a status report to Senior   *Recovery Operations Teams*

Management regarding the operability of the Recovery Center.

031a. Confer with the Emergency Response Team and have

them update Senior Management on the operability of

the Recovery Center.

031b. Provide the intended operations schedule for the coming

week to the Emergency Response Team.

031c. Continue to provide weekly operating schedules to

the Emergency Response Team.

032   When the primary site is operable, go   *Recovery Operations Teams*

to *047*.

Stage 4 – Reconstruction of the Primary Site

Reconstruction Team

033   Take steps to restore processing at the primary   Reconstruction Team

facility; if reconstruction is needed, go to step 033a.

033a. Activate the Rebuilding Team.

033b. Notify appropriate insurance companies and

vendors providing replacement equipment.

033c. Salvage all usable equipment, records and supplies.

033d. Remove all damaged items and arrange for proper disposal.

033e. Make arrangements for acquiring replacement equipment

and supplies.

033f. Obtain backup files and other materials needed for the reconstruction effort.

033g. Arrange for facility cleanup, if required.

033h. Re-establish necessary utilities and environmental equipment. (air conditioning, fire suppression, power conditioning, etc.)

033i. Obtain certification from outside agencies on the acceptability of your environment.

033j. Install replacement equipment.

033k. Confirm functionality of equipment.

033l. Re-install operating system software.

033m. Confirm functionality of system software.

033n. Confirm production system functionality.

033o. Confirm integrity of files.

033p. Inform management of the functionality of the primary site.

034   Establish a work schedule for rebuilding or replacing the primary facility.   Reconstruction Team

034a. Analyze the damage assessment of the data center.

034b. Identify required vendors to assist in the restoration process.

034c. Review reconstruction plans with the Emergency Response Team.

035   Contact contractors regarding need to rebuild/replace   *Reconstruction Team*
the primary facility.

035a. Obtain bids and time estimates.

035b. Analyze costs.

035c. Work through the Emergency Response Team to obtain financial approval for reconstruction expenses.

036   Estimate time to rebuild.   *Reconstruction Team*

036a. Select the most cost-effective bid, taking into account, the cost of operating outside of the Recovery Center.

036b. Negotiate penalties for schedule delays and possible rewards for finishing ahead of schedule.

036c. Adjust completion date estimates to allow for unexpected
       delays.

036d. Select recommended vendors.

036e. Distribute a rebuilding schedule.

037 **Inform the Emergency Response Team of the**   *Reconstruction Team*
       schedules. Inform the Recovery Coordinator of the
       recommended contractors, schedules, potential delays
       and time estimates for returning to the primary site.

038 **Choose contractors.**   *Reconstruction Team*

039 **Rebuild primary facility.**   *Reconstruction Team*

039a. Monitor the reconstruction effort.

039b. Complete the structural area.

039c. Restore utility and security services.

039d. Inform the Emergency Response Team of status on an ongoing basis.

040 **Restore environmental systems.**   *Reconstruction Team*

040a. Re-establish electrical power, air conditioning,
       fire suppression and security entry systems.

040b. Test all systems and backups.

041 **Order equipment.**   *Reconstruction Team*

041a. Obtain the equipment inventory list from
       the Business Continuity Plan.

041b. Order the equipment required. Determine if
       upgrades are desirable or prudent due to obsolescence
       or changed requirements.

041c. Order required cabling.

041d. Obtain delivery dates from all vendors.

041e. Report the installation estimate to the Emergency Response Team.

041f. Oversee vendor installation.

041g. Confirm equipment operation.

041h. Update the Emergency Response Team.

042 Install operating environment. *Standard Operations*

042a. Use backups of the operating system and environmental disks from the Recovery Center, or those stored prior to the disaster at the off-site storage facility.

042b. Procedures for re-installing the operating system will be documented at the Recovery Center.

043 Validate that the operability of the environment *Standard Operations*

is acceptable.

043a. Run selected operating system and production jobs to test operability and the environment at the restored facility.

043b. The restored environment should be successfully processing for 2 to 3 days prior to providing normal service from the primary site.

043c. Inform the Emergency Response Team that the restored site is operational.

Stage 5

044 Schedule the return to the primary facility. *Emergency Response Team*

044a. Determine the rebuilding time provided by the Emergency Reconstruction Team.

044b. Add an appropriate cushion for unexpected delays.

044c. Review operations status reports.

044d. Coordinate the return to accommodate for the normal production schedule.

044e. Schedule for downtime during the move (at least 24 hours).

045 Contact vendors, users, suppliers and clients of the *Senior Management*

scheduled return to the primary facility.

046   Inform the Recovery Center Manager of the   *Recovery Operations Teams*

schedule for moving back to the primary facility.

046a. Determine when the move to the primary facility

will take place.

046b. Add enough time for problems that may arise, and

for normal operations to begin at the primary site.

047   Notify vendors, suppliers, users and clients   *Emergency Response Team*

of your return to the primary facility.

048   Establish a cut-off schedule at the recovery   *Recovery Operations Teams*

center.

048a. Determine when the move will occur.

048b. Establish a cut-off time for changes to the operating

system, data communications, programs, and

production libraries to be backed up and reloaded

at the primary site.

048c. Establish a cut-off time for production processing,

so that data sets can be backed up and reloaded

at the primary site.

049   Perform necessary backups.   *Recovery Operations Teams*

050   Coordinate relocation to primary facility.   *Emergency Response Team*

050a. Arrange for transportation back to the primary

facility and lodging if required.

050b. Arrange for access to the primary site.

051   Prepare the primary facility for production.   *Reconstruction Team*

051a. Perform a safety inspection of the new facility.

051b. Confirm that the environmental and utility systems

are operational.

051c. Review and/or establish facility security procedures.

052 **Move operations to the primary facility.** *Recovery Operations Teams*

052a. Gather all files and documentation for creating

the operating environment. Arrange for their

shipment to the primary facility.

052b. Perform a verification check with the Reconstruction

Team of the site configuration.

052c. Restore and verify the operating system software.

052d. Restore and verify the voice and data communications

software/network.

052e. Inform the Emergency Response Team of the facility's

operating status.

052f. Rebuild JCL (if applicable), programs, software packages and

files at the new facility.

052g. Arrange for backup media to be returned to off-site storage.

052h. Verify that the primary site is fully operational.

052i. Inform the Emergency Response Team of the status.

053 **Restore to normal operations.** *Standard Operations*

053a. Establish production schedules at the new facility.

053b. Backup all files at the Recovery Center.

053c. Restore files at the primary site.

053d. Begin application operations at the primary site.

053e. Resume operating procedures.

053f. Inform the Emergency Response Team of the status.

054 **Discontinue use of the Recovery Center.** *Emergency Response Team*

054a. Take an inventory of the Recovery site and arrange

for the return of equipment and or supplies.

054b. Contact vendors that provided temporary equipment

and supplies.

054c. Discontinue equipment and maintenance agreements

for temporary use at the Recovery Center.

054d. Confirm conversations and agreements in writing.

054e. Arrange for equipment removal and its return to vendors.

054f. Confirm evacuation time with Recovery Center Manager.

054g. Inform Insurance carriers of recovery status.

054h. Discontinue use of temporary recovery staff.

054i. Relocate Company staff to the restored facility.

Stage 6

Emergency Response Team

055   Submit a critique of the Business Continuity Plan.

055a. Review the recovery activity log.

055b. Document your appraisals of those involved

in the recovery process.

055c. List plan deficiencies.

055d. Decide what changes need to be made.

055e. Prepare a report summary for senior management.

055f. Address approved changes with the Recovery Coordinator

to ensure they are incorporated into the plan

Figure 9 - Sample Action Plan — Business Unit

Background Information

The action plan that follows provides instructions, checklists and forms that should be used during and after a declared disaster to aid in the hiring, separation and payment of employees if automated systems are not available.

The following documents are included in this plan:

- Overview of emergency payment options and time recording instructions

- Paper Daily Time Log

- Manager Checklist for New Employees During Payroll System Outage

- I-9 Form with instructions (Form must be approved in Benefits Center within three days of employee starting work)

- Transaction Request Form For Use during Payroll System Outage

- Flow Charts showing process for routing Transaction Request Form and Daily Time Log

    - Hiring New Employees During Emergency

    - Separating Employees During Emergency

    - Employees Who Go on LOA (leave of absence) During Emergency

    - Paper Time Log

File this plan in a location where it can be easily accessed in the event we need to move to emergency operations for a period of time. The above documents may also be accessed at www.*xxxxxxxxxxx*.com/finance/payroll/emergencypreparedness/default.htm.

Options for Completion of Payroll During an Emergency

The Payroll Business Continuity Planning Team has developed a plan in order to complete payroll in the event we have an emergency that disrupts normal payroll and human resources processing. The following is an explanation of the three options that have been developed to ensure we can continue to pay employees during an emergency:

- **Execute the payroll cycle early using the current process** — This can be implemented in the event that employee time has been collected and is ready to be processed. This option does not necessarily mean that payments to employees will occur prior to the pre-determined check date. This decision will be made by the Business Continuity Team based on the circumstances surround the emergency.

- **Execute the payroll cycle late using the current process** — This can be implemented in the event that an unplanned outage has occurred but it has been determined that it will be of a short duration. This option does not necessarily mean that payments to employees will occur after the pre-determined check date. Such a decision will be made by the Business Continuity Team based on the circumstance surround the emergency.

- **Pay employees by implementing the Disaster Payroll Procedure** — This option could be implemented at any time if the above options cannot be implemented. The Disaster Payroll option would be in the form of a pay advance created using the approximate net (take Home) pay for each employee. Once we can return to normal operations, employee appointments and other transactions would be completed as needed, departments would load their employees' correct worked time from paper time forms, the payroll would be generated, a reconciliation process completed to compare the Disaster Payroll with the actual payroll, and any pay differences would be corrected in a subsequent Payroll(s).

Appointment or Change of Status

If there are pending forms that appoint or change the status of an employee, make every effort to get them through the approval routes on a daily basis especially if it appears that we may declare emergency status. If these transactions are not completed prior to the implementation of any of the emergency payroll options described above, they will be handled retroactively once we are no longer in emergency status.

Preparation Prior to Emergency Operations

Should an emergency occur, the Human Resource Management System (HRMS) and Electronic Time Capture systems will likely be unavailable. Each department must have paper time sheets on hand that would be used by employees to record hours worked. A separate time form should be maintained for each bi-weekly pay period. A paper time form is contained in this package and can also be obtained by accessing this web site: www.*xxxxxxx.com*/finance.com/payroll/forms.

In the event that the automated payroll system is unavailable, employee appointments and status changes will need to be communicated to Human Resources using a paper Transaction Request Form which is contained in this package and can also be obtained by accessing this web site: www.*xxxxxxx.com*/finance/payroll/emergency-preparedness.htm. Also contained in this package and above web site is a Manager Checklist for New Employees which will ensure all proper hiring procedures are followed during he emergency period and that new employees are enrolled in benefit plans.

Communication During an Emergency Status

Should Emergency Status be declared, Human Resources and Payroll Services will collaborate and send communications to departments regarding payroll issues including time reporting, employee transactions issues, and deadlines for payrolls. Depending on the type of disaster, the type of communications used may differ from the normal means of communications but we will make use of any and all means available.

Emergency Leave

All nonessential employees will be excused from reporting to work during the time period stated in the Emergency Operations Status Declaration.

Employees who do not work during the emergency period will be granted emergency leave fro their regularly scheduled work hours. Use the emergency leave code to record this time.

Exceptional situations should be brought to the attention of the appropriate administrative office for clarification and approval.

Differential Pay

Evening, Night, and Weekend differential pay will continue during the official emergency period.

Recording Worked Hours

During an official emergency status, essential employees a re scheduled for 12-hour work shifts. Record hours worked as "REG" (Regular). Depending on the employee status, the system will calculate overtime for classified employees who normally earn overtime and compensatory time for Classified Exempt employees who do not earn overtime.

Departments will be responsible for tracking the earning of and the use of Emergency Leave ("EL") for their employees. Use the emergency leave code of EL to record this time used on a future date.

Non-classified employees will receive neither pay nor compensatory time via the time system for hours worked greater than their normal schedule. Departments may have an Emergency :eave policy regarding these employees but it is not to be recorded within the time reporting systems.

DAILY TIME LOG

Employee Name (Print) _____ Week Ending Date _____

Person # _____   WEEK ONE. _____   WEEK TWO _____
HOME DEPARTMENT NUMBER _____
              PAY PERIOD BEGIN DATE. (Sat) _____ THROUGH (Fri) _____

DATES:

NOTE IF ANY HOURS SHOULD BE CHARGED TO ANOTHER ORG ID								
COMP ID OT ORG/ACCT	SAT	SUN	MON	TUE	WED	THU	FRI	TOTAL
_____								
_____								
_____								
_____								

INFORMATION FOR DEPARTMENTS TO RECORD INTO THE HRMS TATT SYSTEM

Employee Signature: _____ Date: _____

Approving Supervisor Signature: _____ Date: _____

ORIGINALS KEPT ON FILE IN HOME DEPT FOR 4 YEARS + CURRENT FISCAL YEAR
EMPLOYEE ENTITLED TO KEEP A COPY

DAILY TIME LOG

Employee Name (Print) _____ Week Ending Date. _____

Person # _____   WEEK ONE: _____   WEEK TWO _____
HOME DEPARTMENT NUMBER· _____
              PAY PERIOD BEGIN DATE (Sat) _____ THROUGH (Fri) _____

DATES:

NOTE IF ANY HOURS SHOULD BE CHARGED TO ANOTHER ORG ID								
COMP ID OT ORG/ACCT	SAT	SUN	MON	TUE	WED	THU	FRI	TOTAL
_____								
_____								
_____								
_____								

INFORMATION FOR DEPARTMENTS TO RECORD INTO THE HRMS TATT SYSTEM

Employee Signature: _____ Date: _____

Approving Supervisor Signature: _____ Date: _____

ORIGINALS KEPT ON FILE IN HOME DEPT FOR 4 YEARS + CURRENT FISCAL YEAR
EMPLOYEE ENTITLED TO KEEP A COPY

Manager Checklist for New Employees During Payroll System Outage

Employee Name: _____

Start Date: _____

Division/Department: _____

Reports To: _____

Manager initiates form for new hires during payroll system outage. Employee and manager utilize this checklist to ensure appropriate new hire setup and orientation. Payroll Services will contact the manager of the hiring department regarding employee payment if normal system functions remain unavailable.

Human Resources

Administration Building, Room 2, 555-1234

_____ Security Clearance (required before employee begins work)

Benefits Center

Administration Building, Room 3, 555-1235

_____ I-9 and Supporting Documentation (Form must be approved in Benefits Center
within three days of employee starting work)

_____ Benefits Elections (medical, dental, etc.)

_____ Visa Clearance (if foreign national) - - Office of International Affairs (555-1236)

_____ W-4 Form

_____ Direct Deposit Form

New Employee Orientation (includes Police and Employee Health Center below)

Administration Building, 5 th Floor

Organizational Development, Training and Recognition, 4 th Floor

_____ Mondays (8-5) Upon Availability Depending on Outage

Police

Administration Building, 1st Floor, 555-1238

_____ ID Badge (for temporary badge until HRMS employee id is assigned)

_____ Keys (as appropriate)

Employee Health Center

Center Building, Broadway Blvd. (4th Street) @ Pine Street, Room 3

555-1238

_____ TB Skin Test

U.S. Department of Justice
Immigration and Naturalization Service

Employment Eligibility Verification

OMB No. 11-5-01-1

INSTRUCTIONS
PLEASE READ ALL INSTRUCTIONS CAREFULLY BEFORE COMPLETING THIS FORM.

Anti-Discrimination Notice. It is illegal to discriminate against any individual (other than an alien not authorized to work in the U.S.) in hiring, discharging, or recruiting or referring for a fee because of that individual's national origin or citizenship status. It is illegal to discriminate against work eligible individuals. Employers **CANNOT** specify which document(s) they will accept from an employee. The refusal to hire an individual because of a future expiration date may also constitute illegal discrimination.

Section 1 - Employee. All employees, citizens and noncitizens, hired after November 6, 1986 must complete Section 1 of this form at the time of hire, which is the actual beginning of employment. The employer is responsible for ensuring that Section 1 is timely and properly completed.

Preparer/Translator Certification. The Preparer/Translator Certification must be completed if Section 1 is prepared by a person other than the employee. A preparer/translator may be used only when the employee is unable to complete Section 1 on his/her own. However, the employee must still sign Section 1.

Section 2 - Employer. For the purpose of completing this form, the term "employer" includes those recruiters and referrers for a fee who are agricultural associations, agricultural employers or farm labor contractors.

Employers must complete Section 2 by examining evidence of identity and employment eligibility within three (3) business days of the date employment begins. If employees are authorized to work, but are unable to present the required document(s) within three business days, they must present a receipt for the application of the document(s) within three business days and the actual document(s) within ninety (90) days. However, if employers hire individuals for a duration of less than three business days, Section 2 must be completed at the time employment begins. **Employers must record: 1)** document title; **2)** issuing authority; **3)** document number, **4)** expiration date, if any; and **5)** the date employment begins. Employers must sign and date the certification. Employees must present original documents. Employers may, but are not required to, photocopy the document(s) presented. These photocopies may only be used for the verification process and must be retained with the I-9. However, **employers are still responsible for completing the I-9.**

Section 3 - Updating and Reverification. Employers must complete Section 3 when updating and/or reverifying the I-9. Employers must reverify employment eligibility of their employees on or before the expiration date recorded in Section 1. Employers **CANNOT** specify which document(s) they will accept from an employee.

- If an employee's name has changed at the time this form is being updated/ reverified, complete Block A.

- If an employee is rehired within three (3) years of the date this form was originally completed and the employee is still eligible to be employed on the same basis as previously indicated on this form (updating), complete Block B and the signature block.

- If an employee is rehired within three (3) years of the date this form was originally completed and the employee's work authorization has expired or if a current employee's work authorization is about to expire (reverification), complete Block B and
  - examine any document that reflects that the employee is authorized to work in the U.S. (see List A or C).
    record the document title, document number and expiration date (if any) in Block C, and complete the signature block.

Photocopying and Retaining Form I-9. A blank I-9 may be reproduced, provided both sides are copied. The Instructions must be available to all persons completing this form. Employers must retain completed I-9s for three (3) years after the date of hire or one (1) year after the date employment ends, whichever is later.

For more detailed information, you may refer to the INS Handbook for Employers, (Form M-274). You may obtain the handbook at your local INS office.

Privacy Act Notice. The authority for collecting this information is the Immigration Reform and Control Act of 1986. Pub. L. 99-603 (8 USC 1324a).

This information is for employers to verify the eligibility of individuals for employment to preclude the unlawful hiring, or recruiting or referring for a fee, of aliens who are not authorized to work in the United States.

This information will be used by employers as a record of their basis for determining eligibility of an employee to work in the United States. The form will be kept by the employer and made available for inspection by officials of the U.S. Immigration and Naturalization Service, the Department of Labor and the Office of Special Counsel for Immigration Related Unfair Employment Practices.

Submission of the information required in this form is voluntary. However, an individual may not begin employment unless this form is completed, since employers are subject to civil or criminal penalties if they do not comply with the Immigration Reform and Control Act of 1986.

Reporting Burden. We try to create forms and instructions that are accurate, can be easily understood and which impose the least possible burden on you to provide us with information. Often this is difficult because some immigration laws are very complex. Accordingly, the reporting burden for this collection of information is computed as follows: 1) learning about this form, 5 minutes; 2) completing the form, 5 minutes; and 3) assembling and filing (recordkeeping) the form, 5 minutes, for an average of 15 minutes per response. If you have comments regarding the accuracy of this burden estimate, or suggestions for making this form simpler, you can write to the Immigration and Naturalization Service, HQPDI, 425 I Street, N.W., Room 4034, Washington, DC 20536. OMB No. 1115-0136.

EMPLOYERS MUST RETAIN COMPLETED FORM I-9
PLEASE DO NOT MAIL COMPLETED FORM I-9 TO INS

Form I-9 (Rev. 11-21-91)N

LISTS OF ACCEPTABLE DOCUMENTS

LIST A		LIST B		LIST C
Documents that Establish Both Identity and Employment Eligibility	**OR**	Documents that Establish Identity	**AND**	Documents that Establish Employment Eligibility

LIST A

Documents that Establish Both Identity and Employment Eligibility

1. U S. Passport (unexpired or expired)

2. Certificate of U.S Citizenship *(INS Form N-560 or N-561)*

3. Certificate of Naturalization *(INS Form N-550 or N-570)*

4. Unexpired foreign passport, with *I-551 stamp or* attached INS Form *I-94* indicating unexpired employment authorization

5. Permanent Resident Card or Alien Registration Receipt Card with photograph *(INS Form I-151 or I-551)*

6. Unexpired Temporary Resident Card *(INS Form I-688)*

7. Unexpired Employment Authorization Card *(INS Form I-688A)*

8. Unexpired Reentry Permit *(INS Form I-327)*

9. Unexpired Refugee Travel Document *(INS Form I-571)*

10. Unexpired Employment Authorization Document issued by the INS which contains a photograph *(INS Form I-688B)*

OR

LIST B

Documents that Establish Identity

1. Driver's license or ID card issued by a state or outlying possession of the United States provided it contains a photograph or information such as name, date of birth, gender, height, eye color and address

2. ID card issued by federal, state or local government agencies or entities, provided it contains a photograph or information such as name, date of birth, gender, height, eye color and address

3. School ID card with a photograph

4. Voter's registration card

5. U.S Military card or draft record

6. Military dependent's ID card

7. U S. Coast Guard Merchant Mariner Card

8. Native American tribal document

9. Driver's license issued by a Canadian government authority

For persons under age 18 who are unable to present a document listed above:

10. School record or report card

11. Clinic, doctor or hospital record

12. Day-care or nursery school record

AND

LIST C

Documents that Establish Employment Eligibility

1. U S social security card issued by the Social Security Administration *(other than a card stating it is not valid for employment)*

2. Certification of Birth Abroad issued by the Department of State *(Form FS-545 or Form DS-1350)*

3. Original or certified copy of a birth certificate issued by a state, county, municipal authority or outlying possession of the United States bearing an official seal

4. Native American tribal document

5. U.S Citizen ID Card *(INS Form I-197)*

6. ID Card for use of Resident Citizen in the United States *(INS Form I-179)*

7. Unexpired employment authorization document issued by the INS *(other than those listed under List A)*

Illustrations of many of these documents appear in Part 8 of the Handbook for Employers (M-274)

Form I-9 (Rev 10/4/00)Y Page 3

U.S. Department of Justice
Immigration and Naturalization Service

OMB No 1115-0136

Employment Eligibility Verification

Please read instructions carefully before completing this form. The instructions must be available during completion of this form. ANTI-DISCRIMINATION NOTICE· It is illegal to discriminate against work eligible individuals. Employers CANNOT specify which document(s) they will accept from an employee. The refusal to hire an individual because of a future expiration date may also constitute illegal discrimination.

Section 1. Employee Information and Verification. To be completed and signed by employee at the time employment begins

Print Name: Last	First	Middle Initial	Maiden Name
Address *(Street Name and Number)*		Apt. #	Date of Birth *(month/day/year)*
City	State	Zip Code	Social Security #

I am aware that federal law provides for imprisonment and/or fines for false statements or use of false documents in connection with the completion of this form.	I attest, under penalty of perjury, that I am (check one of the following) A citizen or national of the United States A Lawful Permanent Resident (Alien # A__ _____) An alien authorized to work until __ / . / __ (Alien # or Admission #) _____
Employee's Signature	Date *(month/day/year)*

Preparer and/or Translator Certification. *(To be completed and signed if Section 1 is prepared by a person other than the employee) I attest, under penalty of perjury, that I have assisted in the completion of this form and that to the best of my knowledge the information is true and correct*

Preparer's/Translator's Signature	Print Name
Address *(Street Name and Number, City, State Zip Code)*	Date *(month/day/year)*

Section 2. Employer Review and Verification. To be completed and signed by employer. Examine one document from List A OR examine one document from List B and one from List C, as listed on the reverse of this form, and record the title, number and expiration date, if any, of the document(s)

List A	OR	List B	AND	List C
Document title _____		_____		_____
Issuing authority _____		_____		_____
Document # _____		_____		_____
Expiration Date *(if any)* __/__/__		__/__/__		__/__/__
Document # _____				
Expiration Date *(if any)* __/__/__				

CERTIFICATION - I attest, under penalty of perjury, that I have examined the document(s) presented by the above-named employee, that the above-listed document(s) appear to be genuine and to relate to the employee named, that the employee began employment on *(month/day/year)* __/__/__ and that to the best of my knowledge the employee is eligible to work in the United States. (State employment agencies may omit the date the employee began employment.)

Signature of Employer or Authorized Representative	Print Name	Title
Business or Organization Name	Address *(Street Name and Number, City, State, Zip Code)*	Date *(month/day/year)*

Section 3. Updating and Reverification. To be completed and signed by employer

A. New Name *(if applicable)*	B. Date of rehire *(month/day/year) (if applicable)*

C. If employee's previous grant of work authorization has expired, provide the information below for the document that establishes current employment eligibility

Document Title _____ Document # _____ Expiration Date (if any) __/__/__

I attest, under penalty of perjury, that to the best of my knowledge, this employee is eligible to work in the United States, and if the employee presented document(s), the document(s) I have examined appear to be genuine and to relate to the individual.

Signature of Employer or Authorized Representative	Date *(month/day/year)*

Form I-9 (Rev 11-21-91)N Page 2

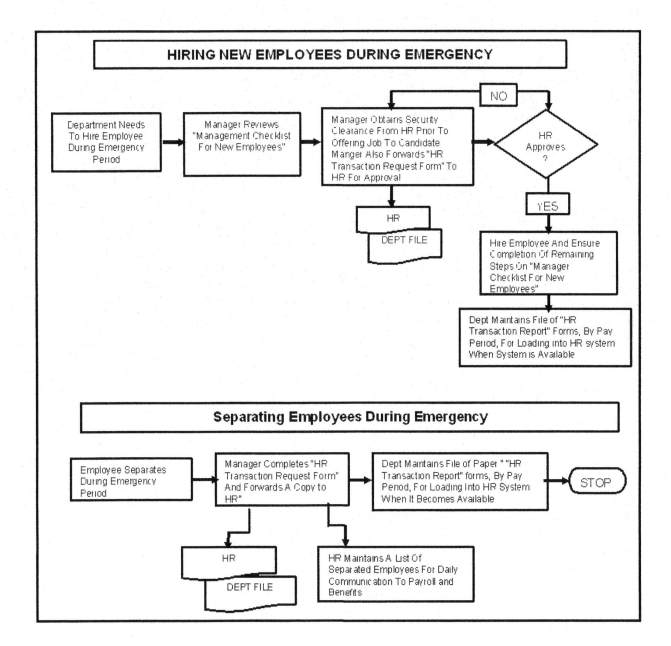

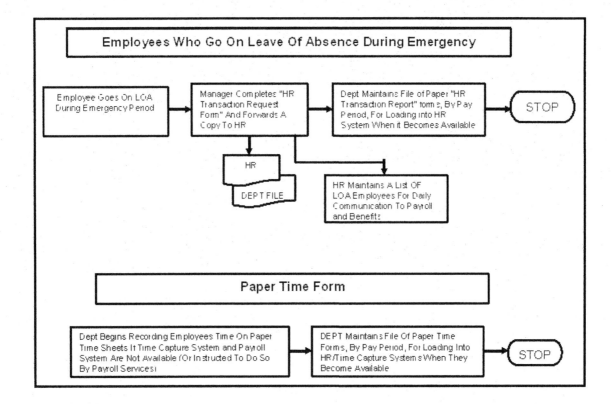

4

PUTTING IT ALL TOGETHER

This chapter documents the guidelines for writing your plan, testing the plan's effectiveness, and finally distributing your plan.

By the end of this chapter you will:

- Understand the guidelines to consider before writing your plan

- Understand the difference between background information and instructional information

- Have developed a general topic outline

- Have chosen the key elements to be included in the appendices

- Understand the different types of the plan testing

- Understand who should be given a copy of the plan

- Have completed Steps 8 thru 10: Documenting your Business Continuity Plan; Testing Your Plan; and, Distributing Your Plan

STEP 8 — DOCUMENTING YOUR BUSINESS CONTINUITY PLAN

Accurate documentation and procedures are very important in any disaster recovery plan. Poorly written procedures can be frustrating and will increase the amount of time to read and understand. Therefore, keep these guidelines in mind when documenting the plan:

- Be specific; do not assume anything.

- Keep all instructions and procedures simple; present one idea at a time.

- Construct brief but effective paragraphs. Use topic sentences to start each paragraph.

- Do not use acronyms; employees may not be familiar with their meaning.

Drafting an outline of the plan's content is a good idea before writing any detailed procedures. A plan outline will help you organize the recovery procedures that need to take place and will identify the important steps to be addressed before your writing commences. Another benefit is that it can ultimately be used as a guideline for creating the table of contents for the final document. A sample *General Topic Outline* is shown in *Figure 9*.

Also consider using a standard format for the Action Plans to ensure consistency throughout the plan. Conformity is especially important if more than one person will be writing the plan. Your plan's content will be made up of primarily two types of information: background information and instructional information; see *Figure 10*.

Background Information

The **background information** might include:

- Purpose of the action plan

- Reference materials (system documentation or other information that should be used)

- Scope of the procedure (location, personnel, equipment required and estimated time to complete the task)

- Identification of forms required to complete the procedure

- Identification of any regulatory policies that must be followed

- Notification list, and/or any specific approvals required

Action Plan

The **action plan**, or instructional information, can be developed on a preprinted form and should be used during the testing process to evaluate and modify the plan. The sample provided in *Chapter 3* is for a data center recovery team, although any department could use the format. Each team section should be formatted so that it can stand alone. This will enable its use if only part of the business is damaged by a disaster. The numbering system should accommodate the insertion of new pages, corrections and ongoing maintenance updates. Remember to precede your action plans with the background information needed to support that specific team's efforts.

Plan Appendices

Business Continuity Plan appendices provide key details not contained in the main body of the plan. The appendices reflect the specific technical, operational, and management contingency requirements of the given system; however, some appendices are frequently found within a separate IT continuity plan. Common Business Continuity Plan appendices include the following:

- Contact information for recovery team personnel.

- Vendor contact information, including offsite storage and alternate site points of contact.

- Standard operating procedures and checklists for system recovery or processes.

- Equipment and system requirements lists of the hardware, software and other resources required to support system operations. Details should be provided for each entry, including model or version number, specifications, and quantity.

- Vendor Service Level Agreements (SLAs), reciprocal agreements with other organizations, and other vital records.

- Description of, and directions to, the alternate site.

- The Business Impact Assessment (BIA), conducted during the planning steps, contains valuable information about the interrelationships, risks, prioritization and impacts to each element of the system. The BIA should be included as an appendix for reference if the plan is activated.

Figure 9 — Sample General Topic Outline for a Business Continuity Plan

- **Introduction** – Overview, the plan's purpose

- **Instructions** – When is the plan to be activated? How it is distributed.

- **Document Organization** – How to use the plan and the way it is organized.

- **Distribution and Amendments** – Who receives the plan, who receives parts of the plan, how to organize future updates, etc.

- **Mission Statement** – Cultural values vital to the plan's mission success.

- **Objectives** – What the plan is to accomplish

- **Scope** – the limits of the plan

- **Assumptions** – assumptions made, i.e., a minimum staff will be available to perform the critical functions of the plan.

- **Declaration Sequence** – Steps taken after a disaster is declared (a flowchart is good for this).

- **Alert/Notification/Activator Procedures**

- **Maintenance and Testing**

- **Outside Support** – List of outside support required, i.e., security, etc.

- **Calling** – Procedures for calling teams, including suggested scripts.

- **Usage** – How will the plan be used?

- **Coordinator** – Responsibilities.

- **Definition of Terms** – Glossary.

- **Skills** – Grouping of available skills if needed during recovery.

- **Application Priorities** – Most critical, order of recovery.

- **Assembly/Command Centers** – Where will teams meet? Where management's command post?

- **Alternate Site** – Hot site, cold site, etc. Backup site location and directions.

- **Communications** – Voice and data end-points for organized restoration.

- **Recovery Teams** – Who. Alternates. Duties.

- **Disaster Scenario** – Potential events.

- **Strategies** – Planned actions for recovery process selection based on severity of outage.

- **Critical Vendors** – Contacts for most important vendors during first 48 hours.

- **Forms** – Sample forms to be used, dependent on disaster, press releases, etc.

- **Preprinted Lists and Samples** – Include vendors, where stored off-site, how long to get printed and delivered.

- **Facility Layout** – Scaled map of functional areas floor space to be used.

- **Call Lists** – List of teams. Who will notify whom? Alternates. List of non-team staff members needing notification. Who calls?

- **Tasks** – Tasks by teams during recovery.

- **Function/Applications** – Prioritized software applications and business functions

- **Computer Operating Procedures** – Probably already exist. Can be referred to and location identified.

- **Site Requirements** – Defines electrical, floor loading, etc. Blueprint-type details recommended. May be separate document.

- **Facilities** – List of all current facilities, off-site storage, alternate site, etc. Driving directions.

- **Personnel** – List of all staff, with skills identified, address, office phone, pagers, home address, home phone, who to notify in case of emergency, and phone number.

- **Vendors** – All doing business with, including phones, addresses, FAX, email, name, etc.

- **Computer Equipment** – Furnishings and equipment by name, number, specialized information.

- **Office Equipment** – Furnishings and other equipment by name, numbers, specialized information.

- **Off-Site Data** – List of all files stored off-site. (Can be used as a checklist in case of disaster).

- **Software** – List of packaged software, vendor's information, outside support, etc.

- **Critical Documents** – List of most important documents for first 48 hours, copies or instructions on where to find them.

- **Supplies** – List of supplies required, especially for the first 48 hours.

- **Travel/Lodging** – How handled: through company, travel agency, etc.

STEP 9 — TESTING YOUR PLAN

Plan testing is essential to your continuity plan. The plan itself should be tested in detail and evaluated regularly — at least once a year. Environmental changes will occur as your organization grows, new products are purchased and new policies and procedures are developed. Time will also erode the staff's memory and critical parts of the plan may be forgotten.

- Other benefits of regular testing include:

- Verifying the compatibility of the off-site recovery location

- Ensuring the adequacy of action plans

- Identifying deficiencies in your existing procedures

- Training of recovery teams, managers and staff

- Demonstrating the ability of your company to recover

- Providing a method for maintaining and updating your plan

Training to support critical skills that may be needed during a disaster is an important part of the testing process. These special skills include first aid; fire extinguishing; evacuation procedures; protection of assets and proprietary information; emergency communication methods; and shutdown procedures for equipment, electricity, water and gas.

> *Note: Training the recovery teams on special and critical skills could be the difference between success and failure during a disaster.*

PREPARATION OF TESTING PROCEDURES

There are several versions of the testing process that can be performed including:

- Checklist testing

- Non-business interruption testing

- Parallel testing

- Business interruption testing.

Checklist Testing

This type of test determines whether adequate supplies are stored at the alternate location, telephone number listings are current, adequate forms are available, and copies of other continuity plans and operations manuals are available. Under this testing scenario, the recovery team reviews the plan and identifies key elements that should be up-to-date and available. The checklist test ensures that each department is in compliance with the requirements of the Business Continuity Plan.

Non-Business-Interruption Test

During this test, your company will simulate a disaster, so your normal business operations are not interrupted. A disaster test plan of this type includes the:

- Purpose of the test

- Objectives

- Timing, scheduling and duration of test

- Participants and their assignments

- Constraints and assumptions.

This test can include the notification procedures, emergency operating procedures and the off-site recovery center. During a non-business interruption scenario, the following areas should be tested adequately: hardware, software, recovery personnel, telecommunications, supplies, forms, all needed documentation, off-site records storage, transportation and utilities.

It may not be practical or economically feasible to perform all the appropriate tasks during this simulated test such as travel, moving equipment, etc. A combination of the checklist test and the non-business interruption test may be more practical for the initial testing, so you can identify required modifications prior to extensive testing.

Parallel Testing

This test can be performed in tandem with the checklist test or non-business interruption test. Under this scenario, historical transactions can be processed against the preceding day's backup at the alternate processing location. All reports normally produced at the alternate location for the current business day should agree with those reports produced at your normal business location.

Business Interruption Testing

This test implements the total Business Continuity Plan. This test is potentially costly and could disrupt your normal business operations, so proceed with caution!

Adequate time must be allotted for this test. For obvious reasons the initial test should not be performed during critical times of your business or data processing cycle, for example, fiscal year-end processing or peak sales cycles. The length of the test should be based on how quickly you would need to recover in a real disaster situation, and can be used to determine where you need to improve the recovery process.

Numerous test scenarios could be planned to identify the type of disaster, the extent of damage, recovery capability, resource availability, backup availability and the time and the duration of the test. Include those individuals with recovery responsibilities, and the time designated for each to perform his or her activities. You may want to initially test only certain portions of the plan, to identify the workability of each part prior to attempting a full test. It may also be best to test after normal business hours or on a weekend to minimize disruption. Once you feel comfortable with the test results, an unannounced test could be done to emphasize preparedness.

Frequency of Test

Recovery testing should be conducted at least annually, or more frequently, depending on the operating environment and criticality of the applications and business functions. If your plan is still relatively new, a quarterly or semiannual test may be in order for the first year.

> Note: Check with senior management to see if any regulatory agency requires that you provide documentation that a disaster recovery plan has been tested successfully.

Evaluating Your Test Results

The Recovery Operations Teams should log events during the testing process that will later assist you in evaluating the results. The Recovery Teams should assess the test results and make modifications that will improve the process and trim valuable minutes or hours. Remember, when dealing with critical applications, every minute cut from the restoration process could translate into thousands of dollars saved. Therefore, it is recommended that you measure the results quantitatively, including:

- The time to perform various actions items

- The accuracy of each activity

- The amount of work completed.

The Checklist Worksheet

Use a checklist form to document procedures to determine if the recovery plan is up-to-date. This process does not require a full test and may be used for review purposes. The checklist should include the following:

- Action items, equipment and procedures to be tested

- A cross-reference to the supporting documentation of the recovery plan

- Testing frequency for each specific task, equipment or procedure

- A place to indicate whether the test was successful or unsuccessful

- A place to record modifications, comments and recommendations for improvement.

You might also test the plan on a sampling basis, such as:

- Telephone numbers of key recovery members

- Vendor's addresses and phone numbers

- Equipment inventory (on and off-site)

- Forms and supplies inventory

- Employee information and assigned recovery tasks

The form found on _Worksheet 8_ can be used to update the action items that were not successful or that need modification.

> Note: You may want to check with internal auditing, risk management or the facilities department to see if they are already performing any of the tests included in your plan.

Worksheet 8 — Sample Test Update and Problem Log

Description of Action Item: Action Item# _____

_____

_____

_____

_____

Team Responsible:

_____

_____

Description of Problem:

_____

_____

_____

_____

_____

Solution:

_____

_____

_____

_____

_____

_____

Date Revised: _____ Mo. _____Day _____Yr.

Team Leader Signature: _____

Worksheet 9 — Sample Test Plan

Test Type: Non-Business Interruption/Alternate Site Processing

Action	Responsible	Date/Time Notes
1. Confirm test schedule with alternate processing location		
2. Arrange for transportation of staff, tapes, documentation and supplies		
3. Review testing procedures and logistics with the recovery team		
4. Confirm arrival of staff, tapes, documentation and supplies		
5. Review backup system configuration with the Recovery Center Manager		
6. Begin documenting exceptions on problem log		
7. Load operating and communication software		
8. Run software installation verification job		
9. Load critical applications		
10. Test console terminal.		
11. Print the predetermined reports.		
12. Erase the critical data after all reports have been printed		
13. Shut down recovery system		
14. Arrange for the shipment of tapes, documentation and supplies back to the home office.		
15. Complete the Test Evaluation Worksheet.		
16. Review the test results with The Recovery Teams and Recovery Center personnel.		
17. Finalize travel plans for return trip home		

The Test Evaluation Form

Your test evaluation form should be used to document the testing procedures and to evaluate the results. Include the following when developing the form:

- The estimated time needed to perform a specific task. This time estimate should be predetermined and correspond to the total time required to be fully operational.

- A description of the task performed. This information is predetermined and is taken from the detailed procedures in the recovery manual.

- A cross-reference to the recovery plan of the procedure tested. This will allow for quick reference to the manual for more information.

- The responsible person or team.

- The time required to complete the specific task.

- The test results (i.e., successful, unsuccessful).

- An area for testing comments, observations, notations, and recommendations for improvement.

Use the form on *Worksheet 10* as a guideline for developing your test evaluation record.

<u>Worksheet 10 — Sample Test Evaluation Form Guideline</u>

Estimated Time	X-Ref	Action	Person Responsible	Actual Time	S/U	Comments

Est. Time = Estimated time to perform the action

Actual Time = Time required to perform the action item.

X-Ref. = Cross reference to the Business Continuity Plan

S = Successful U = Unsuccessful

Action = The action or procedure to be performed during the test

Comments = Observations, notations and recommendations for improvement

Person Responsible = Person responsible for performing the action

Worksheet 11 — Sample Test Record Cover Sheet

The purpose of this record is to provide an ongoing account of the number and types of tests that have been performed. This record may be kept with the Business Continuity Plan, or in a separate Test Manual that contains the detailed test plans and results for each test.

Test Date	Purpose of Test	Comments

STEP 10 — DISTRIBUTING YOUR PLAN

Because of the sensitive nature of the information your plan will contain, it is suggested that only those persons who have been designated as members of the Disaster Recovery Team, or who otherwise play a role in the recovery effort, be given a copy of your continuity plan.

Those receiving a copy of the plan will normally be those who contributed to the information gathering effort. They would most commonly be: Data Center Management, Department Managers, Senior Management and the Plan Coordinator.

Other Considerations:

•   Plan copies should be easily accessible.

•   Several copies of the plan should be stored off-site in a secure location.

•   Key employees may need access to the plan during non-working hours.

•   For ease of maintenance, keep the number of copies at a minimum and number each, noting where each copy is located.

•   If a software program has been used to assist in plan development, store copies of the planning disks and program off-site.

CONGRATULATIONS! —

BUT DON'T LET IT COLLECT DUST

The focus of this chapter is on the importance of maintaining your plan in a constant ready state. A suggested maintenance schedule and maintenance sheets are provided.

By the end of this chapter you will:

- Understand why it is imperative to keep your plan up-to-date

- Understand what should be included to ensure plan effectiveness

- Have developed a schedule of events for plan maintenance

Step 11 — Maintaining Your Plan

To ensure that your plan can be used effectively in case of an emergency, continual updating is imperative and is the responsibility of the plan coordinator. To achieve this goal, the plan coordinator must ensure that:

- Appropriate changes are made to the plan as requested on the maintenance summary sheet; see *Worksheet 16*

- Ongoing plan requirements are completed in accordance with the instructions defined throughout the plan (e.g., file backups).

- Plan testing should take place at least once a year and include:

    1. Verbal contact with all recovery team members to ensure that they understand their roles, should an emergency occur

2.   An audit of the off-site storage facility to ensure that it is being properly maintained

3.   Restoration of critical applications and vital records on the in-house computer system

4.   Recovery of critical applications and vital records on the off-site computer configuration

•   Review the Business Continuity Plan annually for necessary revisions, and have it approved by senior management.

The *Schedule for Plan Review*, found on the following page can be used as a guideline for developing your schedule of events for plan maintenance.

Suggested Schedule for Plan Review

Plan Section	Responsibility	Frequency
Overview, Objectives, Scope And Assumptions	Coordinator	Annual
Distribution List	Coordinator	Quarterly
Testing Procedures	Coordinator	Annually
Emergency Actions Plan	Coordinator	Annually
Recovery Teams	Coordinator, Team Leader/Manager	Quarterly
Vendors	User Liaisons Coordinator	Quarterly
Vital Records	User Liaisons Coordinator	Monthly
Equipment Inventory	User Liaisons Coordinator	Quarterly
Communications	User Liaisons Coordinator	Monthly
Critical Applications / Processes	User Liaisons Coordinator	Monthly
Appendices	Team Leaders / Manager Coordinator	Quarterly

Worksheet 12 — Sample Plan Maintenance Sheet

Page _____ of _____

I. Maintenance Schedule

A. If monthly, identify the month that the maintenance described below represents: _____.

B. If quarterly, check the quarter that the maintenance below represents:

Q1_____ Q2_____ Q3_____ Q4_____

C. If annually, write the annual ranges that the maintenance described below represents

_____ Mo. ___ Yr. to _____Mo. ___ Yr.

II. Maintenance Description

Section	Description	Page	Action Required
_____	_____	____	_____
_____	_____	____	_____
_____	_____	____	_____
_____	_____	____	_____
_____	_____	____	_____
_____	_____	____	_____

Prepared by: _____

Authorized Signature: _____

Date Submitted: _____/_____/_____

APPENDIX A

SAMPLE RISK ASSESSMENT

Instructions: Answer yes or no to each item and then grade each item as a High, Medium or Low priority to rectify. Then estimate the probability of occurrence for each type of threat:

	YES	NO	PRIORITY TO RECTIFY (H/M/L)
Fire Exposure -- Probability of Threat (H/M/L) _____			
1. Is the computer room housed in a building that is fire resistant or non-combustible?			
2. Are the areas surrounding the data center protected from fire?			
3. Are the raised floor tiles and hung ceiling tiles non-combustible?			
4. Can the walls, doors, partitions, floors, furniture and window coverings in the data center resist the spread of fire?			
5. Does the data center have adequate automatic fire extinguishing systems?			
6. Are flammable and otherwise dangerous materials and activities prohibited from the data center and surrounding areas?			
7. Are flammable materials which are used for computer maintenance, stored in small quantities in fire resistance containers?			
8. Are paper and other supplies stored outside the computer area?			
9. Is there fire and smoke detection equipment in the data center? • under the floor? • in the air ducts? • in the ceilings?			

	YES	NO	PRIORITY TO RECTIFY (H/M/L)
10. Are portable fire extinguishers in suitable locations?			
11. Are clear and adequate fire instructions plainly posted?			
12. Is the fire department telephone number clearly posted?			
13. Are the fire alarm switches clearly visible, unobstructed and easily accessible at points of exit?			
14. Can the fire alarm be activated manually?			
15. Does the fire alarm sound: • outside of the data center? • at a guard station? • at the local fire station?			
16. a. Is there an emergency evacuation exit that is different than the main exit? b. Is there an evacuation plan posted?			
17. Is there an adequate supply of clean agents (i.e., water, CO2, inert gas, FM-200, FE-13 etc.) for fire fighting?			
18. Does emergency power shut down the air conditioning?			
19. Are fire and smoke detection equipment checked and tested on a regular basis?			
20. Can emergency crews easily gain access to the data center?			
21. Are fire drills held regularly?			
22. Are tapes and other storage media stored at another location?			
Water Damage Exposure -- Probability of Threat (H/M/L) _____			
1. Are the computers above ground and protected from flooding?			

	YES	NO	PRIORITY TO RECTIFY (H/M/L)
2. Is there a drainage system in the area of the data center?			
3. Can the data center ceiling protect the room from leaks in overhead water pipes?			
4. Is there protection against accumulated rainwater or leaks in the rooftop cooling towers?			
5. Are floor level electrical junction boxes protected?			
Other Natural Disaster Exposures — Probability of Threat (H/M/L)			
1. Can the Department withstand:			
• high winds?			
• tornadoes?			
• earthquakes?			
2. Is the data center and equipment grounded for protection against lightning?			
Electricity and Telecommunications — Probability (H/M/L) ____			
1. Are generators and transformers located outside of the data center?			
2. Is there an emergency lighting system in the data center?			
3. Is the data center equipped with power conditioning to protect against power surges?			
4. Are there backup power sources available?			
5. Do alternate voice and data transmission services exist?			
6. Is there protection from unauthorized access to the telecommunications system?			
7. Is there a shutdown checklist provided in case of emergency?			
8. Are the machine operators familiar with shut down procedures?			

	YES	NO	PRIORITY TO RECTIFY (H/M/L)
Air Conditioning — Probability (H/M/L) _____			
1. Is the air conditioning system and power supply for the data center separate from the rest of the building?			
2. Is there backup air conditioning available?			
3. Is the fresh air intake located above ground level and away from smoke stacks and sources of combustible dust and gas?			
4. Are air conditioning and emergency shutoff switches linked?			
5. Are switches easily accessible?			
Facility Access Control -- Probability of Threat (H/M/L) _____			
1. Are there procedures to guard against vandalism, sabotage, and unauthorized intrusion?			
2. Are there windows that can be broken to gain access to the data center?			
3. Are there procedures for data center personnel to handle: • unauthorized intruders? • bomb threats? • notifying the local police?			
4. Are security devices checked and tested on a regular basis?			
5. Do any of the following pose a threat to the data center based on their proximity to the data center? • loading ramps? • cafeteria or workshops? • storage areas? • outside walls? • power panels? • heavy usage of electrical equipment?			

	YES	NO	PRIORITY TO RECTIFY (H/M/L)
6. Are there access controls during regular and off-hours: • to other departments? • to the computer room?			
General Housekeeping -- Probability of Threat (H/M/L) _____			
1.Is the data center kept clean and orderly?			
2. Are food and beverages prohibited in the data center or at least confined to a designated area?			
3. Is smoking banned in the data center?			
4. Is there a media cleaning and rotation schedule?			
5. Is there adequate lightning for all areas?			
Organization and Personnel -- Probability (H/M/L/) _____			
1. Are there company personnel responsible for data center security?			
2. Does management have procedures for dealing with disgruntled employees?			
3. Have recovery teams been selected in the event of a disaster?			
4. Are there disaster plans in place?			
Backup and Recovery -- Probability of Threat (H/M/L) _____			
1. Is there an inventory of critical files?			
2. Have specific task assignments been made for al personnel for recovery strategy procedures?			
3. Are duplicate data files and copies of all computer programs stored at another location?			
4. Is a backup computer available? If so, can it adequately handle critical processing requirements?			
Magnetic Tapes and Disks -- Probability (H/M/L) _____			
1. Is there an inventory list of tapes and disks?			

	YES	NO	PRIORITY TO RECTIFY (H/M/L)
2. Do procedures exist for controlling tape and disk storage?			
3. Is the alternate storage site protected from fire, flood, dust, vandalism, theft, etc.			
4. Is access to the library restricted to authorized personnel only?			

APPENDIX B

RISK ANALYSIS CHECKLIST

Instructions: The designated planning team member(s) can use this template as a guideline when performing the Risk Analysis. It may also be used as a Disaster Prevention Checklist.

I.   **THE SITE**

Examine the general topography, site location and layout.

A.   Low lying lands -- flood risk

B.   Hilltop site -- lightning risk

C.   Access roads and transportation systems

    1.   Alternate routes

    2.   Proximity of public services -- fire department, etc

    3.   Proximity to rail and waterways

    4.   Site boundaries

    5.   Access restrictions for large vehicles

D.   Access risk from neighboring companies and others

    1.   Toxic and corrosive products

    2.   Explosive and flammable products

    3.   Pressure groups, activists

E.   Access risk from neighboring community

    1.   Local population

    2.   Land development, construction

    3.   Planning constraints for future development

F.   Hazard from geographic location

    1.   Railway

2.   Airport flight path

3.   Public right of way

4.   Weekend security

G.   Access control

1.   Effective barriers at entrance

2.   Perimeter fencing

3.   Fence patrolled, lit, and protected by closed circuit TV

4.   Intruder detection

5.   Affected by weather

6.   Procedures to deal with visitors

7.   Staff encouraged to challenge unidentified personnel on site

II.   THE BUILDING

Inspect the building interior and exterior to determine the following:

A.   Age and type of construction

B.   Type of fire protection and suppression

C.   Is the fire protection system zoned?

D.   Shared building occupancy

1.   Other occupants

2.   Nature of trade or business

3.   Locations within the building

4.   Access, parking, storage concerns

E.   Building environment

1.   Close to manufacturing

2.   Traffic on site

3.   Building walls forming site boundary

4.   Routing for telecommunications

F.   Location of computer room

1.   Access for equipment

    2.   Occupancy of building above, below or immediately adjacent to computer room

    3.   Location of air conditioning outlets

    4.   Fire escapes and external walkways

G.   Facility cabling system

H.   Curtains, furnishings fire retardant?

I.   Access arrangements to roof

III. THE DATA CENTER

A.   Fire detection and control systems

    1.   Smoke detectors; type and locations

    2.   Adequacy of fire extinguishers; check expiration dates

    3.   Manual or automatic control devices

    4.   Control devices separate from rest of building

    5.   Staff training on use

    6.   Equipment tests

    7.   Equipment maintenance

    8.   Instructions for arming systems

    9.   Evacuation procedures

    10.   Ventilation fans working

    11.   Accessibility for fire crew

B.   Walls, floors and partitions

    1.   Construction

    2.   Bare concrete slabs sealed

    3.   Fire door rating

    4.   False ceiling

    5.   Anti-static floor finish

    6.   Floor jacks properly bonded to slab

    7.   Unnecessary services through ceiling

    8.   Floor and ceiling cables in good condition

9.   Evidence of past problems

C. Air Conditioning

1.   Redundancy

2.   Filter specifications appropriate for installed equipment

3.   Date of last particle count and results

4.   Condition of filters

5.   Maintenance schedule

6.   Connection to uninterrupted power supply

7.   Controlled by fire detection system

8.   Air conditioner alarms linked to security

D.   Water sensor in the floor void

1.   Water detection linked to security

2.   Floor clear of trash, unwanted pipes and cables

E.   Power system

1.   Earth grounds properly connected

2.   False floor electrically bonded

3.   Breakers adequately labeled

4.   Cleaning and utility supplies clearly marked

5.   Uninterruptible Power Supply in continuous operation

6.   If normally bypassed, how often is a full-load test performed

7.   Frequency of test on emergency generator

8.   History of power supply problems

9.   Emergency off buttons installed

10.   Utility supplies available when operating on standby operation

11.   Generator fuel supply adequate

12.   Days/hours of fuel for continuous operation

13.   Generator cooling radiator full

14.   History of operational problems with generator, for example, noises, vibration, exhaust outlet direction

E.   Adequate access to controls

F.   Intruder alarm linked to security

IV.   OPERATIONS AND SECURITY

A.   Review basic practices and procedures.

1.   Satisfactory backup procedures

2.   How and where are the backups stored

3.   Full documentation with backup tapes

4.   Internal/external audit checks

5.   Complete and accurate Operations Manuals

6.   Formal security policy

7.   Is policy being observed?

8.   Proper use and auditing of passwords

9.   Disposal of sensitive output

10.   Security log examined regularly

11.   Dial-in access permitted/controlled

V.   HOUSEKEEPING AND PERSONNEL

A.   Inspect general area and speak with personnel.

1.   Adequate lighting in all areas

2.   Smoking and eating banned in computer room

3.   Evidence of noncompliance?

4.   Clean desk policy

5.   Media cleaned/rotated regularly

6.   Background checks on new hires

7.   Regular and constructive performance evaluations

8.   General level of staff morale

9.   Proper induction and termination procedures

10.   Clearly defined and documented procedures to deal with fire, bomb threats and other emergencies

11.   Responsibilities split so that fraud cannot be perpetrated

12.   without collusion

13.   Casual practices, such as leaving sensitive material unlocked

14.   Personnel taking security seriously

15.   Fire escape routes clearly marked and provided with emergency lighting

APPENDIX C

GUIDELINES FOR DEVELOPING

YOUR DATA SHEETS

Vital Records Inventory List

The purpose of the vital records inventory is to record the location of vital and critical records. This form should include:

1. The record name and ID#

2. The record description (stockholder information, policies, incorporation documentation, etc.)

3. Building or area where the record is stored

4. Type of storage (master #, pack #, backup procedures, frequency, etc.)

5. Record classification (vital, important, useful)

Computer Hardware and Software Inventory List

The purpose of this form is to document the inventory of computer equipment and software. A separate form should be used for critical equipment and software that would be necessary in a disaster situation.

1. Vendor name, address, telephone number

2. Type of system (mainframe, micro, mini, local area network, etc.)

3. Serial number, model and manufacturer

4. Operator and user terminals

5. Other peripheral equipment and network devices

6. Critical applications supported by the configuration (include program name and version)

7. Recovery time (the time required to replace the equipment)

8. Memory and special features including storage requirements

9. Description of the use of the equipment

10.   Leasing information

11.   Insurance information

If the recovery time is longer than acceptable, a backup solution should be considered for those systems necessary in a disaster situation.

Communications Inventory List

The communications inventory listing should document the entire communications network.

1.   Circuit name and description

2.   Vendor

3.   Baud rate

4.   Protocol used (asynch, bisynch, etc.)

5.   Type of service (dedicated, non-dedicated)

6.   Interface with computer (e.g., type of multiplexer)

7.   Interface with devices (e.g., dial-up)

8.   Terminating device type and location

9.   Model number

If your continuity plan will depend on dial-up to a "hot-site" from end users, your plan should also include:

1.   Hot-site modem number and alternate number

2.   Name of local and long distance phone carrier; include customer support numbers

3.   Instructions on how to connect to hot-site

4.   Telephone number for users to call for technical support

If your continuity plan requires the communications vendor to switch existing lines to a remote location that has switching arrangements, then your plan should include:

1.   A description and diagram of the switching process

2.   Telephone number for vendor activation of plan

3.   Password or other information required by the vendor for plan activation

4.   Any additional instructions, documentation or phone numbers needed for implementation and use.

Vendor List

The vendor list should list vendors in the order they need to be called in the recovery process.

1. Name

2. Address

3. Business and emergency contact phone numbers

4. Contact person and title

5. Description of the service or product supplied

Office Supplies

The purpose of this form is to list the critical office supply inventory needed for recovery.

1. Part number

2. Description

3. Vendor names, addresses, telephone numbers and contact name

4. Turnaround time between ordering and receiving

5. Quantity stored on and off-site

Forms Inventory

The purpose of this listing is to document all forms needed for recovery.

1. Form number and last revision date

2. Description

3. Vendor names, addresses, telephone numbers and contact name

4. Turnaround time between ordering and receiving

5. Quantity of forms stored on and off-site

If the turnaround time is longer than acceptable, consider storing a larger quantity off-site.

Documentation Inventory List

The purpose of the documentation inventory list is to record the inventory of critical documentation manuals. The list should identify the type of documentation such as computer logs, operating systems software manuals, user manuals, software documentation, accounting manuals, polices, procedures, etc., and should also include:

1.   The storage location

2.   Number of copies

3.   Procedures for obtaining the documentation

Critical Telephone Numbers

The purpose of this form is to list telephone numbers that may be important in the recovery process.

1.   Emergency 911

2.   Fire department

3.   Police department

4.   Ambulances

5.   Hospitals

6.   Red Cross

7.   Civil Defense

8.   Post Office

9.   Banks

10.   Alternate Site

11.   Computer Vendor

12.   Telephone company

13.   Regulatory agencies

14.   Utility companies

15.   Media

16.   Courier services

17.   Contractors

18.   Temporary personnel agencies

Call Log

The call log can be used to record all telephone calls made during the disaster and can be referred to for reviewing internal and external communications. Consider separate logs for incoming and outgoing calls.

1.   Date

2.   Name of employee who places or receives call

3.   Company name, contact and telephone number

4.   Comments (notations, response)

Employee Call List

The master call list is a list of employee telephone numbers. It should contain:

1.   Position/Job title

2.   Employee name

3.   Employee address

4.   Employee home telephone number

5.   Recovery team title and function

Employee Backup List

The employee backup list identifies backup employees for each position within the company. Certain key personnel may not be available and therefore backups should be identified.

1.   Position/Job title

2.   Name of employee currently assigned to position

3.   Name(s) of backup or temporary employees who can fill the position,

Notification Checklist

The purpose of the notification checklist is to list the responsibilities for calling staff, vendors and others. Each team should be assigned specific parties to contact. The checklist should include:

1.   Primary contact name (employee, vendor, civil authorities, etc.)

2.   Backup contact name

3.   Date and time of contact

4.   Comments and responses

Skills Inventory List

The skills inventory list should identify the skills of each employee. This list will permit recovery operations to commence if certain key employees (Recovery Team Members) cannot get to their assigned task and there is no backup available. This list should include:

1.   Job description and title

2.   Employee name

3.   Types of skills required for this function (bookkeeping, word processing, programmer, etc.)

4.   Skill rating such as, above average, average, needs development, cannot perform the defined skill

Telephone Inventory Listing

The telephone inventory listing documents the existing telephone systems - voice and data communications that are important to daily operations. This listing should include:

1.   Location, department, vendor name

2.   Instrument description (single-line, multi-line, speakerphone, etc.)

3.   Model and serial number

4.   Quantity of each

Off-Site Storage Inventory

The purpose of the off-site inventory list is to document all materials stored off-site.

1.   Name, address, and telephone number of off-site storage facility

2.   Media description (tape, floppies, disk cartridge, etc.)

3.   Software application documentation

4.   Operating system software and manuals

5.   Special forms inventory

6.   Supplies inventory (stock paper, extra disks, office supplies)

7.   Company operating manuals

8.   Business Continuity Plan

9.   Other critical documentation and materials necessary in a disaster situation

Off-Site Processing Information

The purpose of this form can be used to plan for, or document the alternate site processing specifications. The form should identify the site as a "hot-site" (computer configurations already installed) or as a ""cold-site," (computers must be relocated and installed). Also include:

1.   Name, address and telephone number of facility.

2.   Facility description (e.g., number of rooms, type of construction, square footage, parking)

3.   Electrical specifications and environmental specifications (air conditioning, elevators, humidity).

4.   Fire protection ratings and specifications

5.   Security

6.   Communications specifications for voice and data

7.   System configurations installed

8.   System configurations required that are not installed (explain method of obtaining

9.   equipment) (correct number)

10.   Cost of using facility (subscription fees, notification charges, hourly rates, etc.)

11.   Notification requirements

12.   Transportation and lodging information

13.   Estimated time for relocate and restore

Insurance Policy List

The insurance policy list documents current policies and should include:

1.   Name of insurance company, policy number and effective dates of coverage

2.   Type of policy coverage (business interruption, loss of data, etc.) and limits of coverage

3.   Contact person and telephone number.

APPENDIX D

BUSINESS CONTINUITY GLOSSARY

The definitions in this glossary were developed by the Disaster Recovery Journal, (www.drj.com), in conjunction with Disaster International, DRI, 2003. Used with the permission of DRJ.

ACTIVATION: The implementation of business continuity capabilities, procedures, activities and plans in response to an emergency or disaster declaration; the execution of the recovery plan.

ALERT: Notification that a potential disaster situation exists or has occurred; direction for recipient to stand by for possible activation of disaster recovery plan.

ALTERNATE SITE: An alternate operating location to be used by business functions when the primary facilities are inaccessible. (1) Another location, computer center or work area designated for recovery. (2) Location, other than the main facility, that can be used to conduct business functions. (3) A location, other than the normal facility, used to process data and/or conduct critical business functions in the event of a disaster. *SIMILAR TERMS*: Alternate Processing Facility, Alternate Office Facility, Alternate Communication Facility, Backup Location, Recovery Site.

ALTERNATE WORK AREA: Office recovery environment complete with necessary office infrastructure (desk, telephone, workstation, and associated hardware, communications, etc.); also referred to as Work Space or Alternative work site.

APPLICATION RECOVERY: The component of Disaster Recovery that deals specifically with the restoration of business system software and data, after the processing platform has been restored or replaced. SIMILAR TERMS: Business System Recovery.

BACKUP GENERATOR: An independent source of power, usually fueled by diesel or natural gas.

BUSINESS CONTINUITY INSTITUTE (BCI, www.thebci.org): A not-for-profit organization that offers certification and educational offerings for business continuity professionals.

BUSINESS CONTINUITY PLANNING (BCP): Process of developing advance arrangements and procedures that enable an organization to respond to an event in such a manner that critical business functions continue with planned levels of interruption or essential change. *SIMILAR TERMS*: Contingency Planning, Disaster Recovery Planning.

BUSINESS CONTINUITY PROGRAM: An ongoing program supported and funded by executive staff to ensure business continuity requirements are assessed, resources are allocated and, recovery and continuity strategies and procedures are completed and tested.

BUSINESS CONTINUITY STEERING COMMITTEE: A committee of decision-makers, business owners, technology experts and continuity professionals, tasked with making strategic recovery and continuity planning decisions for the organization.

BUSINESS IMPACT ANALYSIS (BIA): The process of analyzing all business functions and the effect that a specific disaster may have upon them. 1) Determining the type or scope of difficulty caused to an organization should a potential event identified by the risk analysis actually occur. The BIA should quantify, where possible, the loss impact from both a business interruption (number of days) and a financial standpoint. SIMILAR TERMS: Business Exposure Assessment, Risk Analysis

BUSINESS INTERRUPTION: Any event, whether anticipated (e.g., public service strike) or unanticipated (e.g., blackout) which disrupts the normal course of business operations at an organization location.

BUSINESS INTERRUPTION COSTS: The costs or lost revenue associated with an interruption in normal business operations.

BUSINESS INTERRUPTION INSURANCE: Insurance coverage for disaster related expenses that may be incurred until operations are fully recovered after a disaster.

BUSINESS RECOVERY COORDINATOR: An individual or group designated to coordinate or control designated recovery processes or testing. *SIMILAR TERMS*: Disaster Recovery Coordinator

BUSINESS RECOVERY TIMELINE: The chronological sequence of recovery activities, or critical path that must be followed to resume an acceptable level of operations following a business interruption. This timeline may range from minutes to weeks, depending upon the recovery requirements and methodology.

BUSINESS RESUMPTION PLANNING (BRP): TERM Currently Being Reworked. SIMILAR TERMS: Business Continuity Planning, Disaster Recovery Planning

BUSINESS RECOVERY TEAM: A group of individuals responsible for maintaining the business recovery procedures and coordinating the recovery of business functions and processes. SIMILAR TERMS: Disaster Recovery Team

BUSINESS UNIT RECOVERY: The component of Disaster Recovery which deals specifically with the relocation of a key function or department in the event of a disaster, including personnel, essential records, equipment supplies, work space, communication facilities, work station computer processing capability, fax, copy machines, mail services, etc. *SIMILAR TERMS*: Work Group Recovery.

CALL TREE: A document that graphically depicts the calling responsibilities and the calling order used to contact management, employees, customers, vendors, and other key contacts in the event of an emergency, disaster, or severe outage situation.

CERTIFIED BUSINESS CONTINUITY PROFESSIONAL (CBCP): The Disaster Recovery Institute International (DRI International), a not-for-profit corporation, certifies CBCPs and promotes credibility and professionalism in the business continuity industry. Also offers MBCP (Master Business Continuity Professional) and ABCP (Associate Business Continuity Professional).

CHECKLIST EXERCISE: A method used to exercise a completed disaster recovery plan. This type of exercise is used to determine if the information such as phone numbers, manuals, equipment, etc. in the plan is accurate and current.

COLD SITE: An alternate facility that already has in place the environmental infrastructure required to recover critical business functions or information systems, but does not have any pre-installed computer hardware, telecommunications equipment, communication lines, etc. These must be provisioned at time of disaster. *SIMILAR TERMS*: Shell Site; Backup Site; Recovery Site; Alternate Site.

COMMUNICATIONS RECOVERY: The component of Disaster Recovery, which deals with the restoration, or rerouting of an organization's telecommunication network, or its components, in the event of loss. *SIMILAR TERMS*: Telecommunications Recovery, Data Communications Recovery

COMPUTER RECOVERY TEAM: A group of individuals responsible for assessing damage to the original system, processing data in the interim, and setting up the new system.

CONSORTIUM AGREEMENT: An agreement made by a group of organizations to share processing facilities and/or office facilities, if one member of the group suffers a disaster. SIMILAR TERMS: Reciprocal Agreement.

COMMAND CENTER: Facility separate from the main facility and equipped with adequate communications equipment from which initial recovery efforts are manned and media-business communications is maintained. The management team uses this facility temporarily to begin coordinating the recovery process and its use continues until the alternate sites are functional.

CONTACT LIST: A list of team members and/or key players to be contacted including their backups. The list will include the necessary contact information (i.e., home phone, pager, cell, etc.) and in most cases be considered confidential.

CONTINGENCY PLANNING: Process of developing advance arrangements and procedures that enable an organization to respond to an event that could occur by chance or unforeseen circumstances.

CONTINGENCY PLAN: A plan used by an organization or business unit to respond to a specific systems failure or disruption of operations. A contingency plan may use any number of resources including workaround procedures, an alternate work area, a reciprocal agreement or replacement resources.

CONTINUITY OF OPERATIONS PLAN (COOP): A COOP provides guidance on the system restoration for emergencies, disasters, mobilization, and for maintaining a state of readiness to provide the necessary level of information processing support commensurate with the mission requirements/priorities identified by the respective functional proponent. This term traditionally is used by the Federal Government and its supporting agencies to describe activities otherwise known as Disaster Recovery, Business Continuity, Business Resumption or Contingency Planning.

CRATE & SHIP: A strategy for providing alternate processing capability in a disaster, via contractual arrangements with an equipment supplier, to ship replacement hardware within a specified time period. *SIMILAR TERMS*: Guaranteed Replacement, Drop-Ship, Quick Ship.

CRISIS: A critical event, which, if not handled in an appropriate manner, may dramatically impact an organization's profitability, reputation or ability to operate.

CRISIS MANAGEMENT: The overall coordination of an organization's response to a crisis, in an effective, timely manner, with the goal of avoiding or minimizing damage to the organization's profitability, reputation or ability to operate.

CRISIS MANAGEMENT TEAM: A crisis management team will consist of key executives as well as key role players (i.e. media representative, legal counsel, facilities manager, disaster recovery coordinator, etc.) and the appropriate business owners of critical organization functions

CRISIS SIMULATION: The process of testing an organization's ability to respond to a crisis in a coordinated, timely, and effective manner, by simulating the occurrence of a specific crisis.

CRITICAL FUNCTIONS: Business activities or information that could not be interrupted or unavailable for several business days without significantly jeopardizing operation of the organization.

CRITICAL INFRASTRUCTURE: Systems whose incapacity or destruction would have a debilitating impact on the economic security of an organization, community, nation, etc

CRITICAL RECORDS: Records or documents that, if damaged or destroyed, would cause considerable inconvenience and/or require replacement or recreation at considerable expense.

DAMAGE ASSESSMENT: The process of assessing damage, following a disaster, to computer hardware, vital records, office facilities, etc., and determining what can be salvaged or restored and what must be replaced.

DATA BACKUPS: The back up of system, application, program and/or production files to media that can be stored both on and/or offsite. Data backups can be used to restore corrupted or lost data or to recover entire systems and databases in the event of a disaster. Data backups should be considered confidential and should be kept secure from physical damage and theft.

DATA BACKUP STRATEGIES: Those actions and backup processes determined by an organization to be necessary to meet its data recovery and restoration objectives. Data backup strategies will determine the timeframes, technologies, media and offsite storage of the backups, and will ensure that recovery point and time objectives can be met.

DATA CENTER RECOVERY: The component of Disaster Recovery that deals with the restoration, at an alternate location, of data centers services and computer processing capabilities. SIMILAR TERMS: Mainframe Recovery, Technology Recovery.

DATA RECOVERY: The restoration of computer files from backup media to restore programs and production data to the state that existed at the time of the last safe backup.

DATABASE REPLICATION: The partial or full duplication of data from a source database to one or more destination databases. Replication may use any of a number of methodologies including mirroring or shadowing, and may be performed synchronous, asynchronous, or point-in-time depending on the technologies used, recovery point requirements, distance and connectivity to the source database, etc. Replication can if performed remotely, function as a backup for disasters and other major outages. *SIMILAR TERMS*: File Shadowing, Disk Mirroring.

DISK MIRRORING: Disk mirroring is the duplication of data on separate disks in real time to ensure its continuous availability, currency and accuracy. Disk mirroring can function as a disaster recovery solution by performing the mirroring remotely. True mirroring will enable a zero recovery point objective. Depending on the technologies used, mirroring can be performed synchronously, asynchronously, semi-synchronously, or point-in-time. *SIMILAR TERMS*: File Shadowing, Data Replication, Journaling.

DECLARATION: A formal announcement by pre-authorized personnel that a disaster or severe outage is predicted or has occurred and that triggers pre-arranged mitigating actions (e.g., a move to an alternate site).

DECLARATION FEE: A one-time fee, charged by an Alternate Facility provider, to a customer who declares a disaster. NOTE: Some recovery vendors apply the declaration fee against the first few days of recovery. 1) An initial fee or charge for implementing the terms of a recovery agreement or contract. SIMILAR TERMS: Notification Fee.

DESK CHECK: One method of testing a specific component of a plan. Typically, the owner or author of the component reviews it for accuracy and completeness and signs off.

DISASTER: A sudden, unplanned calamitous event causing great damage or loss. (1) Any event that creates an inability on an organizations part to provide critical business functions for some predetermined period of time. (2) In the business environment, any event that creates an inability on an organization's part to provide the critical business functions for some predetermined period of time. (3) The period when company management decides to divert from normal production responses and exercises its disaster recovery plan. Typically signifies the beginning of a move from a primary to an alternate location. *SIMILAR TERMS*: Business Interruption; Outage; Catastrophe.

DISASTER RECOVERY: Activities and programs designed to return the entity to an acceptable condition. (1) The ability to respond to an interruption in services by implementing a disaster recovery plan to restore an organization's critical business functions.

DISASTER RECOVERY OR BUSINESS CONTINUITY COORDINATOR: The Disaster Recovery Coordinator may be responsible for overall recovery of an organization or unit(s). SIMILAR TERMS: Business Recovery Coordinator.

DISASTER RECOVERY INSTITUTE INTERNATIONAL (DRI INTERNATIONAL, www.drii.org): A not-for-profit organization that offers certification and educational offerings for business continuity professionals.

DISASTER RECOVERY PLAN: The document that defines the resources, actions, tasks and data required to manage the business recovery process in the event of a business interruption. The plan is designed to assist in restoring the business process within the stated disaster recovery goals.

DISASTER RECOVERY PLANNING: The technological aspect of Business Continuity Planning. The advance planning and preparation that is necessary to minimize loss and ensure continuity of the critical business functions of an organization in the event of disaster. SIMILAR TERMS: Contingency Planning; Business Resumption Planning; Corporate Contingency Planning; Business Interruption Planning; Disaster Preparedness.

DISASTER RECOVERY SOFTWARE: An application program developed to assist an organization in writing a comprehensive disaster recovery plan.

DISASTER RECOVERY TEAMS (Business Recovery Teams): A structured group of teams ready to take control of the recovery operations if a disaster should occur.

ELECTRONIC VAULTING: Electronically forwarding backup data to an offsite server or storage facility. Vaulting eliminates the need for tape shipment and therefore significantly shortens the time required to move the data offsite.

EMERGENCY: A sudden, unexpected event requiring immediate action due to potential threat to health and safety, the environment, or property.

EMERGENCY PREPAREDNESS: The discipline that ensures an organization, or community's readiness to respond to an emergency in a coordinated, timely, and effective manner.

EMERGENCY PROCEDURES: A plan of action to commence immediately to prevent the loss of life and minimize injury and property damage.

EMERGENCY OPERATIONS CENTER (EOC): A site from which response teams/officials (municipal, county, state and federal) exercise direction and control in an emergency or disaster.

ENVIRONMENT RESTORATION: Recreation of the critical business operations in an alternate location, including people, equipment and communications capability.

EXECUTIVE / MANAGEMENT SUCCESSION: A predetermined plan for ensuring the continuity of authority, decision-making, and communication in the event that key members of senior management suddenly become incapacitated, or in the event that a crisis occurs while key members of senior management are unavailable.

EXERCISE: An activity that is performed for the purpose of training and conditioning team members, and improving their performance. Types of exercises include: Table Top Exercise, Simulation Exercise, Operational Exercise and Mock Disaster.

FILE SHADOWING: The asynchronous duplication of the production database on separate media to ensure data availability, currency and accuracy. File shadowing can be used as a disaster recovery solution if performed remotely, to improve both the recovery time and recovery point objectives. *SIMILAR TERMS*: Data Replication, Journaling, Disk Mirroring.

FINANCIAL IMPACT: An operating expense that continues following an interruption or disaster, which as a result of the event cannot be offset by income and directly affects the financial position of the organization.

FORWARD RECOVERY: The process of recovering a database to the point of failure by applying active journal or log data to the current backup files of the database.

HAZARD OR THREAT IDENTIFICATION: The process of identifying situations or conditions that have the potential to cause injury to people, damage to property, or damage to the environment.

HIGH AVAILABILITY: Systems or applications requiring a very high level of reliability and availability. High availability systems typically operate 24x7 and usually require built in redundancy built-in redundancy to minimize the risk of downtime due to hardware and/or telecommunication failures.

HIGH-RISK AREAS: Heavily populated areas, particularly susceptible to high-intensity earthquakes, floods, tsunamis or other disasters, for which emergency response may be necessary in the event of a disaster.

HOT SITE: An alternate facility that already has in place the computer, telecommunications, and environmental infrastructure required to recover critical business functions or information systems.

HUMAN THREATS: Possible disruptions in operations resulting from human actions. (i.e., disgruntled employee, terrorism, blackmail, job actions, riots, etc.)

INCIDENT COMMAND SYSTEM (ICS): Combination of facilities, equipment, personnel, procedures and communications operating within a common organizational structure with responsibility for management of assigned resources to effectively direct and control the response to an incident. Intended to expand, as situation requires larger resources, without requiring new, reorganized command structure. (NEMA Term)

INCIDENT MANAGER: Commands the local EOC reporting up to senior management on the recovery progress. Has the authority to invoke the local recovery plan.

INCIDENT RESPONSE: The response of an organization to a disaster or other significant event that may significantly impact the organization, its people or its ability to function productively. An incident response may include evacuation of a facility, initiating a disaster recovery plan, performing damage assessment, and any other measures necessary to bring an organization to a more stable status.

INTEGRATED TEST: A test conducted on multiple components of a plan, in conjunction with each other, typically under simulated operating conditions

INTERIM SITE: A temporary location used to continue performing business functions after vacating a recovery site and before the original or new home site can be occupied. Move to an interim site may be necessary if ongoing stay at the recovery site is not feasible for the period of time needed or if the recovery site is located far from the normal business site that was impacted by the disaster. An interim site move is planned and scheduled in advance to minimize disruption of business processes; equal care must be given to transferring critical functions from the interim site back to the normal business site.

INTERNAL HOT SITE: A fully equipped alternate processing site owned and operated by the organization.

JOURNALING: The process of logging changes or updates to a database since the last full backup. Journals can be used to recover previous versions of a file before updates were made, or to facilitate disaster recovery, if performed remotely, by applying changes to the last safe backup. *SIMILAR TERMS*: File Shadowing, Data Replication, Disk Mirroring.

LAN RECOVERY: The component of business continuity that deals specifically with the replacement of LAN equipment and the restoration of essential data and software in the event of a disaster. *SIMILAR TERM*: Client/Server Recovery.

LINE REROUTING: A short-term change in the routing of telephone traffic, which can be planned and recurring, or a reaction to an outage situation. Many regional telephone companies offer service that allows a computer center to quickly reroute a network of dedicated lines to a backup site.

LOSS REDUCTION: The technique of instituting mechanisms to lessen the exposure to a particular risk. Loss reduction involves planning for, and reacting to, an event to limit its impact. Examples of loss reduction include sprinkler systems, insurance policies and evacuation procedures.

LOST TRANSACTION RECOVERY: Recovery of data (paper within the work area and/or system entries) destroyed or lost at the time of the disaster or interruption. Paper documents may need to be requested or re-acquired from original sources. Data for system entries may need to be recreated or reentered.

MISSION-CRITICAL APPLICATION: An application that is essential to the organization's ability to perform necessary business functions. Loss of the mission-critical application would have a negative impact on the business, as well as legal or regulatory impacts.

MOBILE RECOVERY: A mobilized resource purchased or contracted for the purpose of business recovery. The mobile recovery center might include: computers, workstations, telephone, electrical power, etc.

MOCK DISASTER: One method of exercising teams in which participants are challenged to determine the actions they would take in the event of a specific disaster scenario. Mock disasters usually involve all, or most, of the applicable teams. Under the guidance of exercise coordinators, the teams walk through the actions they would take per their plans, or simulate performance of these actions. Teams may be at a single exercise location, or at multiple locations, with communication between teams simulating actual 'disaster mode' communications. A mock disaster will typically operate on a compressed timeframe representing many hours, or even days.

NATURAL THREATS: Events caused by nature that have the potential to impact an organization.

NETWORK OUTAGE: An interruption in system availability resulting from a communication failure affecting a network of computer terminals, processors and/or workstations.

OFF-SITE STORAGE: Alternate facility, other than the primary production site, where duplicated vital records and documentation may be stored for use during disaster recovery.

OPERATIONAL EXERCISE: One method of exercising teams in which participants perform some or all of the actions they would take in the event of plan activation. Operational exercises, which may involve one or more teams, are typically performed under actual operating conditions at the designated alternate location, using the specific recovery configuration that would be available in a disaster.

OPERATIONAL IMPACT ANALYSIS: Determines the impact of the loss of an operational or technological resource. The loss of a system, network or other critical resource may affect a number of business processes.

OPERATIONAL TEST: A test conducted on one or more components of a plan under actual operating conditions.

PLAN ADMINISTRATOR: The individual responsible for documenting recovery activities and tracking recovery progress.

PEER REVIEW: One method of testing a specific component of a plan. Typically, the component is reviewed for accuracy and completeness by personnel (other than the owner or author) with appropriate technical or business knowledge.

PLAN MAINTENANCE PROCEDURES: Maintenance procedures outline the process for the review and update of business continuity plans.

RECIPROCAL AGREEMENT: Agreement between two organizations (or two internal business groups) with basically the same equipment/same environment that allows each one to recover at each other's site.

RECOVERY: Process of planning for and/or implementing expanded operations to address less time-sensitive business operations immediately following an interruption or disaster. 1) The start of the actual process or function that uses the restored technology and location.

RECOVERY PERIOD: The time period between a disaster and a return to normal functions, during which the disaster recovery plan is employed.

RECOVERY SERVICES CONTRACT: A contract with an external organization guaranteeing the provision of specified equipment, facilities, or services, usually within a specified time period, in the event of a business interruption. A typical contract will specify a monthly subscription fee, a declaration fee, usage costs, method and amount of testing, termination options, penalties and liabilities, etc.

RECOVERY STRATEGY: An approach by an organization that will ensure its recovery and continuity in the face of a disaster or other major outage. Plans and methodologies are determined by the organizations strategy. There may be more than one methodology or solution for an organizations strategy. Examples of methodologies and solutions include, contracting for Hot-site or Cold-site, building an internal Hot-site or Cold-site, identifying an Alternate Work Area, a Consortium or Reciprocal Agreement, contracting for Mobile Recovery or Crate and Ship, and many others.

RECOVERY POINT OBJECTIVE (RPO): The point in time to which systems and data must be recovered after an outage (e.g. end of previous day's processing). RPOs are often used as the basis for the development of backup strategies, and as a determinant of the amount of data that may need to be recreated after the systems or functions have been recovered.

RECOVERY TIME OBJECTIVE (RTO): The period of time within which systems, applications or functions must be recovered after an outage (e.g. one business day). RTOs are often used as the basis for the development of recovery strategies, and as a determinant as to whether or not to implement the recovery strategies during a disaster situation. *SIMILAR TERMS*: Maximum Allowable Downtime.

RESPONSE: The reaction to an incident or emergency to assess the damage or impact and to ascertain the level of containment and control activity required. In addition to addressing matters of life safety and evacuation, Response also addresses the policies, procedures and actions to be followed in the event of an emergency. 1) The step or stage that immediately follows a disaster event where actions begin as a result of the event having occurred. *SIMILAR TERMS*: Emergency Response, Disaster Response, Immediate Response and Damage Assessment.

RESTORATION: Process of planning for and/or implementing procedures for the repair or relocation of the primary site and its contents, and for the restoration of normal operations at the primary site.

RESUMPTION: The process of planning for and/or implementing the restarting of defined business operations following a disaster, usually beginning with the most critical or time-sensitive functions and continuing along a planned sequence to address all identified areas required by the business. (1) The step or stage after the impacted infrastructure, data, communications and environment has been successfully reestablished at an alternate location.

RISK: Potential for exposure to loss. Risks, either man-made or natural, are constant. The potential is usually measured by its probability in years.

RISK ASSESSMENT / ANALYSIS: Process of identifying the risks to an organization, assessing the critical functions necessary for an organization to continue business operations, defining the controls in place to reduce organization exposure and evaluating the cost for such controls. Risk analysis often involves an evaluation of the probabilities of a particular event.

RISK MITIGATION: Implementation of measures to deter specific threats to the continuity of business operations, and/or respond to any occurrence of such threats in a timely and appropriate manner.

SALVAGE & RESTORATION: The process of reclaiming or refurbishing computer hardware, vital records, office facilities, etc. following a disaster.

SIMULATION EXERCISE: One method of exercising teams in which participants perform some or all of the actions they would take in the event of plan activation. Simulation exercises, which may involve one or more teams, are performed under conditions that at least partially simulate 'disaster mode.' They may or may not be performed at the designated alternate location, and typically use only a partial recovery configuration.

STANDALONE TEST: A test conducted on a specific component of a plan, in isolation from other components, typically under simulated operating conditions.

STRUCTURED WALKTHROUGH: One method of testing a specific component of a plan. Typically, a team member makes a detailed presentation of the component to other team members (and possibly non-members) for their critique and evaluation.

SUBSCRIPTION: Contract commitment that provides an organization with the right to utilize a vendor recovery facility for processing capability in the event of a disaster declaration.

SYSTEM DOWNTIME: A planned or unplanned interruption in system availability.

TABLE TOP EXERCISE: One method of exercising teams in which participants review and discuss the actions they would take per their plans, but do not perform any of these actions. The exercise can be conducted with a single team, or multiple teams, typically under the guidance of exercise facilitators.

TEST: An activity that is performed to evaluate the effectiveness or capabilities of a plan relative to specified objectives or measurement criteria. Types of tests include: Desk Check, Peer Review, Structured Walkthrough, Standalone Test, Integrated Test, and Operational Test.

TEST PLAN: A document designed to periodically exercise specific action tasks and procedures to ensure viability in a real disaster or severe outage situation.

UNINTERRUPTIBLE POWER SUPPLY (UPS): A backup supply that provides continuous power to critical equipment in the event that commercial power is lost.

VITAL RECORD: A record that must be preserved and available for retrieval if needed.

WARM SITE: An alternate processing site, which is equipped with some hardware, and communications interfaces, electrical and environmental conditioning that is only capable of providing backup after additional provisioning, software or customization, is performed.

WORKAROUND PROCEDURES: Interim procedures that may be used by a business unit to enable it to continue to perform its critical functions during temporary unavailability of specific application systems, electronic or hard copy data, voice or data communication systems, specialized equipment, office facilities, personnel, or external services. *SIMILAR TERMS*: Interim Contingencies.

Links to a number of other Business Continuity and related glossaries may be found at http://www.rothstein.com/links/links.html under the sub-heading "Glossaries."

APPENDIX E

SELECTED BUSINESS

CONTINUITY ARTICLES

PITCHING PREPAREDNESS

by Philip Jan Rothstein, FBCI

When it comes to contingency planning, what does an organization really have to show for its' money and effort? For those sophisticated enough to realize it, the much-maligned yet ubiquitous three-inch red binder simply does not cut it any more. More and more companies are looking for tangible, quantifiable results from their business continuity efforts and expenditures.

KEY POINTS

- Justify on tangible results, not emotions

- Point out specific, direct benefits

- Recognize top management may have other conflicts

- Speak top management's language

Business continuity and disaster recovery have gained somewhat in the eyes of top corporate management since the start of the 1990's. As the industry has slowly evolved from what could almost have been called a 'black art' to something starting to resemble a disciplined science, basic business principles have begun to become increasingly relevant. These principles include cost-benefit analysis, project planning and management, accountability and auditability.

In many organizations disaster recovery has been exempt from these 'sound business practices' for at least three reasons:

- The image of disaster recovery has been as much emotionally charged as rationally driven, with commitments and decisions driven by the presence or lack of either a 'champion' or of a traumatic event to spur action

- The skills and abilities of many struggling contingency planners to effectively present and document their requirements, accomplishments and efforts and to successfully build business cases for resource or dollar expenditures have been limited at best

- The tools, methodologies and processes of the business continuity/disaster recovery industry have been evolving rapidly but even now exhibit omissions or inconsistencies.

Consider if you will the engineering discipline as a model for the contingency planning discipline. Engineers have resources and structures which have evolved over decades: professional standards; certifications of competence; proven and accepted processes, practices and tools; standardized methodologies; specific areas of specialization as well as core competencies; extensive data bases and information sources; budgeting, planning and forecasting tools and templates; standardized models; and so forth. These are well documented for the engineer, with numerous case studies and examples to relate to in any new situation. By comparison, The contingency planner, by comparison, has limited resources and structures to rely on.

MAKING A CASE

For top management to dedicate funds and resources to contingency planning, more than a demonstrable need must be shown: some basic, common-sense questions must be answered to put this effort in perspective with other organization investments, priorities and initiatives. In other words, the contingency planner must learn to compete for scarce resources and funding. To be successful, the contingency planner must be able to succinctly and precisely answer these questions:

- What are we getting for our money and time?

- How can we be assured that it will be effective?

- What are the consequences if we do not do this at all, or put it off for a while?

- What are the alternatives?

The first of these questions is often the most daunting in that the classic outcome of even the most effective contingency plan is, bluntly, theoretical: the ability to successfully recover and continue business operations without unacceptable damage or loss from an event which may or may not ever occur. To typical executive management, this is unlikely to be a compelling argument in the face of day-to-day crises and, as often as not, business continuity/disaster recovery are considered back-burner projects which do not ever achieve viability.

Second, the likelihood that the investment will pay off in a contingency capability that will actually work when it is called upon is a question that may be difficult to answer, short of an actual disaster. The contingency planner's job is, in part, to provide top management with specific, credible evidence to support any claims of effectiveness and, even more important, to be totally candid about any constraints, weaknesses, exceptions or ongoing vulnerabilities. A contingency planner who sets out to convince top management that their efforts will result in a "bulletproof" recovery capability is going to lack credibility.

Third, the contingency planner must realize that top management is constantly juggling priorities, crises and demands from many sources. No matter how compelling the argument for investment in business continuity, top management is always going to consider the option of doing little or nothing. The contingency planner's job is to objectively spell out the consequences of inaction, delay or minimal investment in unemotional terms.

Fourth, the contingency planner must be honest with themselves as much as with top management about alternatives. Given the myriad conflicting demands for corporate resources, it is quite possible that one of those alternatives may prove to be more appropriate. Executive management is likely to be most impressed by the contingency planner who presents a business case with viable, carefully analyzed options.

INVESTMENT JUSTIFICATION

To the top corporate executive, funding a project or, more properly making an ongoing investment in business continuity, should happen for at least two reasons:

- As a function of the organization's mission and commitment to that mission: "how can we continue to deliver on our mission in the event something terrible happens to us?"

- What measurable, tangible, direct results are the organization gaining from this investment?

In practice, the first issue is thorny enough — after all, many organizations are either not precise in their mission or not truly focused on an explicit mission statement. Even where the mission is clear, the top executive has to also consider the impact on and perceptions of stakeholders and other interested parties including customers, employees, stockholders, suppliers, competitors, the public and press — as well as legal and regulatory implications.

The second issue is where many contingency planners may have neither the acumen, experience or ammunition to present a business case and to gain management support. The typical contingency planner learns, through education and experience, to develop (and hopefully exercise and maintain) the contingency plan. "Disaster Recovery 101" does not prepare them for the rigors of justifying their work (or, in some cases, their continued employment) through executive presentations. Unfortunately, without this latter skill, they may never get the opportunity to become effective at contingency planning. Top management invariably expects any significant request for resources or expenditures to be accompanied by a business justification demonstrating measurable, tangible results. The contingency planner is in fact selling something inherently intangible, unmeasurable and indirect.

LEARNING FROM EXPERIENCE

In one client organization, a line manager recently presented top executive management with a professional, carefully constructed proposal for enterprise-wide business continuity. Recent "near-misses" had heightened awareness and concern. The proposal addressed extending contingency planning beyond the data center to at least the most vital business units of this medium-sized, New England-based service organization.

Top management's response was lukewarm. Business continuity was viewed as desirable but, as is often the case, "urgent business priorities" had to be handled first. As most contingency planning professionals have learned, this is a management euphemism for "that's nice, but don't waste our time." Clearly, this manager had not struck a responsive chord in the presentation.

Working with the disheartened manager, it was learned that this client organization's top management emphasized consistent, timely achievement of specific, measurable objectives. Service quality and consistency of service delivery were core business planning issues. The manager agreed with the consultant's recommendation to center the pitch on these themes.

A second meeting with the executive group was requested and an alternate strategy developed. Instead of emphasizing recovery from disruption as the exclusive objective, enhanced recoverability was acknowledged as just one benefit. The principal benefits of the proposed business continuity investment were specifically focused on the service quality and service delivery.

GETTING GRAPHIC

Since Executive management regularly employed graphic service delivery reports as management tools, the second presentation utilized these commonly accepted graphic and report formats. First, "near-miss" events over the prior thirty months were briefly summarized. Then, two variations of the graphs and reports were presented:

*   Actual service delivery over the prior thirty months

*   Estimated service delivery if "near-miss" events during that period had escalated into "real" disruptions.

Since the "near-miss" events were based on actual experience, they were believable. They included a train derailment on the freight line behind the company's offices, involving a chemical spill (which had actually occurred about five miles up the line); an electrical power outage lasting four hours from a transformer failure; a one-day work shutdown because of heavy snow and icing; a half-day work stoppage; a half-day closure because of flooding in the area; and, a two-hour total telephone outage when a truck knocked out an overhead line.

RE-FOCUS IMPROVES FOCUS

The next step was to present a detailed service delivery and bottom-line analysis for a single month, based on a specific, hypothetical event. The event chosen was one which actually had occurred recently to a comparably sized competitor: a fire in their corporate offices. The anticipated bottom-line impact in this case was close to a million dollars although it was emphasized that the estimates were rough and that a business impact assessment would help to identify the likely exposure to loss as well as the sensitivity of various business functions in more specific terms.

At this point in the presentation, executive management began asking perceptive questions. Already, the level of interest was noticeably higher than during the previous presentation. The first line of questioning was about the business impact assessment: how long it would take, what kind of effort, what would be the outcome and results. The consensus was that this assessment should be made a near-term priority.

The second line of questioning was about protecting the corporate offices: what kind of preventive or containment measures might be prudent, who should have that accountability, and what to do if, despite these efforts, a disruption occurred. The executive management group delegated this aspect to the corporate facilities manager and directed him to report back in one month with initial recommendations.

The focus was then turned to development of a company-wide continuity plan. No longer was the focus on disasters: the conversation centered on service quality and the bottom line. The issues of employee safety and payroll obligations were raised. The line manager was now in the enviable position of executive management pressing him for an effective business continuity program   a solution to a problem they had not previously recognized.

READY FOR RESULTS

This time, the line manager was better prepared. He pulled out a time line which summarized at a high level a prudent project plan, with specific, achievable deliverables. Each deliverable was accompanied by a manpower estimate and cost estimate   expense and capital. One of the executives immediately noticed that the time line and expenditures were configured to mesh with fiscal year objectives as well as two vital, current corporate initiatives. The ensuing discussion centered around funding and staffing, but, unlike the first presentation, the theme was "who will do the best job?" rather than "we can't spare the people."

The outcome of this session was encouraging. The line manager was given a clear mandate to proceed with planning and implementation of a corporate-wide business continuity program. Executive management designated specific resources on which he could draw and invited him to requisition other resources as needed. They agreed to act promptly on a corporate policy statement the line manager was to draft. They agreed on specific objectives and timeframes:

- a specific project work plan with milestones, budget, staffing plan and deliverables, within one month

- a draft corporate policy statement for adoption by the executive committee, within one month

- within one month, identification and prioritization of significant vulnerabilities and threats and a near-term action plan to reduce these vulnerabilities

- publication of a periodic newsletter beginning within three months

- quarterly executive briefings

- within six months, identification and prioritization of mission-critical business operation and essential resources

- within eight months, an action plan to minimize the identified vulnerabilities and threats of disruption

- within nine months, a strategy for continuity of business operations in the face of the identified threats

- within fifteen months, a target date and action plan with specific objectives for an initial corporate continuity exercise.

The line manager was elated with the outcome of this session, although he felt that some of the timeframes could have been more aggressive. On the other hand, it was agreed that the tasks were achievable and he was explicitly granted access to the necessary resources.

THE BOTTOM LINE

Developing a contingency plan is enough of a challenge. The art of eliciting top management support is not taught in "Disaster Recovery 101," yet it is assumed that the contingency planner is versed in the essential skills. Too many contingency planners learn the hard way that top management expects a persuasive business justification before investing funds or resources in contingency planning before "paying for preparedness."

This article originally appeared in Contingency Planning & Management Magazine.

WHY ASSESS?

By Philip Jan Rothstein, FBCI

> *Few businesses can survive for long by investing in projects without examining their justification, whether through a structured process or informally. Yet, it is not uncommon for a business continuity or disaster recovery program to evolve without a rational business basis. Why is this?*

In theory, a contingency plan should be based on three key factors which are objectively weighed in a Business Impact Assessment (BIA): threats, vulnerabilities, and exposure to loss.

In practice, the most ominous threats may not always be apparent; vulnerabilities may be concealed; and, exposure to loss difficult to quantify. But, the most common themes observed in organizations with contingency programs not based on impact assessments are (1) not grasping the relevance of the impact assessment process in the first place or, bluntly (2) "no glory."

The first point is difficult enough to resolve. The contingency/recovery program is so easily justified on emotional grounds ("we've got to get the data center back within twelve hours or we're out of business!") that it is easy to gloss over the objectivity introduced by a BIA or by an Applications Impact Analysis, which concentrates on the impact to business operations resulting from computer applications outages.

The second point is often more nettlesome. The outcome of a BIA is knowledge which may or may not impact the bottom line and therefore does not typically inspire outrageous salary reviews. Also, the BIA process often looks like an obstacle to implementing the contingency plan "everybody knows we need right away" rather than a valuable guide.

A CASE STUDY

The risks to this oversight are theoretically obvious yet almost invariably overlooked, as we recently observed in a Midwestern manufacturing company. Their data center was protected by a reasonably thorough and remarkably well exercised disaster recovery program. Disaster recovery had evolved over a period of seven years without a BIA or applications impact assessment at any time.

Management confidence in MIS recoverability was high and, in fact, appeared justified. The first "ultimate" test a real disaster resulting from a burst water main resulted in a successful data center recovery with critical applications operational within ten hours and full restoration of data center services at an alternate site within eighteen hours of declaration, well within the 24-hour target window.

That was the good news. The bad news was that within 96 hours, several business functions were in shambles. Bottom-line losses were edging toward the seven-figure level. Sales and Customer Service were increasingly encountering embarrassing errors.

Could a BIA and applications impact analysis have prevented this fiasco? Probably. First, management had never objectively examined the direct impact on Sales and Customer Service of an extended computer outage. Both areas could not effectively cope with the continuing influx of new business plus inquiries and changes to old business, without computer access for even one day. Data restored from the previous night's backup tapes resulted in inconsistencies with transactions already under way. New orders and changes coming in to Sales and Customer Service while the data center recovery was going on were completely out of synch with the computerized data being restored.

LESSONS LEARNED

This unfortunate company learned the hard way that their targeted 24-hour data center disaster recovery window did not meet their business needs. Of course, the balance could as easily have gone the opposite way an actual business need which did not justify the 24-hour recovery window.

This was observed in another manufacturing company, spending over $12,000 each month on a data center hot site recovery program. This was subsequently replaced with a $1,500 per month cold site agreement when a BIA and Applications Impact analysis revealed that the worst-case, bottom-line impact of a two-week computer outage would likely be less than what was spent annually on the hot site!

The lessons learned are simple:

*   Any contingency program not based on an objective analysis of threats, vulnerabilities and exposure to loss is unlikely to meet the true needs of the organization

*   A BIA does not have to be a complex, lengthy process to be effective the "80-20" rule often applies

*   A BIA ensures that the contingency planning investment is not wasted or, even worse, ineffective when it is most needed.

SLOW-MOTION DISASTER

by Philip Jan Rothstein, FBCI

For residents and businesses in the northeastern United States, with the possible exception of snowplow operators, the winter of 1995-96 was a bummer. Curiously, from the business continuity perspective recurring, disagreeable weather (as opposed to short-term, extreme weather such as tornadoes, hurricanes or blizzards) does not seem to fall into the "disaster" category.

What is a "disaster," anyway? It is any event which substantially disrupts "business as usual." Fires, earthquakes, power failures, extended computer outages or network failures are, in general, no-brainers when it comes to identifiable disaster causes. The winter of 1995-96, on the other hand, brought the northeastern United States one humongous storm preceded and followed by "only" harsh storms, icing, and other less than desirable conditions. Curiously, despite near-record snow accumulations, ski resort businesses in the region were apparently affected adversely by the storms which seemed to appear almost every Friday, preventing skiers from getting to the slopes on prime ski weekends. Talk about your "no-win" situation!

LOOKING BACK

Management executives of one consulting client, a medium-sized manufacturing company, had the insight to examine the overall impact of this past winter on their business. They had based their continuity program on a business impact assessment which concluded that they could reasonably tolerate an outage generally up to two business days without substantial impact. When they looked back at this past winter, they discovered some interesting facts which caused them to reexamine their assumptions:

1. On seven separate occasions, they had met their explicit criteria for declaring a disaster and had not done so;

2. On three occasions, there was direct, bottom-line dollar impact in the mid- to high-five figures; and,

3. Aggregate dollar losses directly attributable to yucky weather approached one million dollars within a sixty-day period.

Looking deeper, they discovered several contributing factors which they had not previously considered "disaster" related:

1.   Quantifiable lost productivity directly attributable to storm days or early dismissals was dwarfed by easily overlooked, indirect productivity losses such as re-doing project plans; rescheduling meetings; revising commitments; a rise in sick and personal days; employees talking about (or worrying about) the weather instead of their work; and, re-doing work which became obsolete because of weather delays.

2.   The only time their contingency plan was explicitly consulted in the course of the winter was in early January when the staff business continuity planner was snowed in at home by the biggest storm of the season and wisely decided to sit down and read over the plan rather than to shovel his driveway.

3.   Overtime made necessary more than a month after the worst of the storms cost the company over $100,000 additional.

In considering productivity loss, morale is a factor which should not be ignored — a senior manager in this company observed that many employees seemed lethargic and unfocused which he attributed in part to "cabin fever." She noted half-jokingly yet painfully accurate that her impression was that the entire company was "...in a funk" and exhibited many characteristics which, in an individual, could be considered symptoms of clinical depression. Keeping in mind that this particular company is somewhat enlightened and sophisticated in addressing business continuity, what can the rest of us learn from their situation (aside from moving to a warmer climate)?

1.   A "disaster" can sneak up on you and your organization — it does not always grab your attention; some "disasters" are only recognizable in hindsight.

2.   A contingency plan — and, in particular the plan's activation criteria — must be flexible enough to address circumstances which had not even been considered when the plan was designed or tested.

3.   The disaster declaration process needs checks and balances to ensure that the organization does not fall into the trap of denial. In assessing business impact, the indirect and intangible losses may far outweigh direct losses.

MANAGING MANAGEMENT:

A CASE STUDY

by Philip Jan Rothstein, FBCI

Planners developing and maintaining a contingency plan can learn the hard way that top management's lack of support, commitment and funding can be a project killer.

Developing, implementing, testing and maintaining a contingency/recovery plan can certainly be a challenging and even a frustrating process. More and more contingency planners are learning the hard way that the toughest piece of the project may have little directly to do with actual development and implementation that gaining, cultivating and maintaining top management's support, commitment and funding can be a project killer.

Working in a consultative relationship with one client recently, I had the opportunity to observe and alter the dynamics of this relationship first-hand. Having worked with dozens of organizations wrestling with wavering top management commitment to disaster recovery, it was easy to spot the symptoms. Be warned that spotting the symptoms early does not always ensure a successful outcome.

The particular client is a successful, growing, medium-sized, financial services organization with close to a thousand employees in two principal locations. The MIS organization has had a disaster recovery plan in place for about four years. It is tested about twice yearly, although not aggressively, and generally well maintained. Top management had become complacent about MIS recovery: they assumed that MIS would be able to fully recover from virtually any disruption in a matter of hours and had paid little attention to disaster recovery over the past three or four years. A request from MIS for renewal of the multi-year hot site agreement, with a significant cost increase, had brought disaster recovery into top management's arena.

The Chief Financial Officer had been the mentor for disaster recovery during the last iteration, around four years ago. At that time, he supported MIS' commitment to contingency planning and encouraged appropriate funding. Since that time, much had changed: the company had not only more than doubled in size and revenue, but had acquired two smaller companies which now depended heavily on the corporate MIS operation. Technologically, the company had moved from mainframe, terminal-based systems to client-server applications and to numerous local area networks with varying degrees of sophistication, protection and control.

At a recent, semimonthly management committee meeting which was my introduction to the organization, the Chief Information Officer presented a synopsis of the planned enhancements to the MIS disaster recovery plan. He discussed the additional complexity of recovering the client/server and LAN environments, as well as the business risks associated with increased dependency on telecommunications and external networks. He recommended expanding the scope to address interim processing strategies for critical business units to cope while MIS was recovering the infrastructure, as well as to deal with data integrity during the disruption. He suggested further broadening the contingency planning scope to work-area recovery and to the telecommunications network, eventually to include voice recoverability. His presentation was professional, yet nontechnical.

The initial reaction from the dozen or so senior managers present was stunned silence. The Chief Operating Officer finally broke the ice by questioning the need for any recovery program at all, since, "... after all, we've never had a disaster." One of the business unit managers expressed concern with any additional work or expense for his already overloaded group. The Chief Financial Officer, who had been a supporter of disaster recovery in the past, noted the company's tenuous financial position as a result of the recent acquisitions and expressed concern with the additional expense. The Chief Information Officer, quite pale by this time, quietly offered to go back to his staff and reexamine the issues and options.

WHAT WENT WRONG?

It quickly became apparent to this consultant that the problem in this organization was not in contingency planning - the MIS disaster recovery plan could be characterized as at least adequate, if not aggressive. The trap this company fell into is a common one: operating on the basis of assumed expectations. The CEO, CFO, business unit managers and others outside MIS made several assumptions about MIS and its ability to recover from a disruption. Since, the last round of justification for a hot site contract more than four years ago, MIS had not communicated explicitly to clarify or contradict these assumptions. While the CIO's presentation and recommendations were probably on target, his audience was unable to reconcile these recommendations with the assumptions they had been living with for four years.

The biggest assumption was that MIS was somehow populated by wizards who could instantaneously, miraculously and painlessly handle any crisis that comes their way and have the business units operational within a few hours; the reality was that, at best, recovery from a major disruption would take 30-36 hours. The second assumption was that MIS had automatically integrated all of the diverse technologies and platforms which had popped up over the past four years into the disaster recovery program; the reality was that MIS did not even implement or operate many of these platforms. The third assumption was that, no matter what the cause or scope of disruption, MIS would recover all data accurately to the point of failure; the reality was that, at best, recovery would be to the prior night's backup and, most probably, to a point at least three to four nights prior.

The moral to this story is that with some delicate negotiation and outside consulting assistance, the top management of this enterprise eventually saw the light and not only approved the CIO's proposal but established a working committee to address company-wide business continuity. Along the way, among the lessons this CIO painfully learned were:

- *Don't rely on top management's, clients' or other stakeholders' assumptions about your ability to deliver salvation from disruption* — document explicit disaster recovery service level agreements which spell out the limitations as well as the promises.

- *Communicate regularly to stakeholders any technological, business or operational changes which impact disaster recoverability* — don't wait until there is no longer a practical option or alternative, or until business management has already acted on the basis of out-of-date assumptions.

- *Present disaster recovery options, constraints and alternatives to business unit managers and to top management early in their decision cycles* — don't wait until they are committed to a course of action which impairs disaster recoverability.

"ALMOST" DISASTERS

by Philip Jan Rothstein,FBCI

> Sometimes, a "disaster" can sneak up on an organization unrecognized. This article offers tips to avoid this pitfall.

Anybody involved in disaster recovery should not find it difficult to recite their own "top-ten" list of favorite disaster causes. They might include natural disasters such as floods, hurricanes, earthquakes or blizzards; external events such as power or communications failures; technological disruptions like computer crashes or network outages; or, facility events like fires. If one were to conduct a careful analysis of corporate 'disasters' over the past decade, one would find that there are numerous disaster causes or potential causes which are largely overlooked. For example:

- a major financial organization experienced a seven-figure dollar loss because of a single data base corrupted by a programmer who updated a production program without following production signoff or turnover standards or procedures.

- a large metropolitan hospital irrevocably lost their entire pharmacy data base including current patient information when a disk crash led them to discover that the backup tapes they had been consistently producing nightly for over two years were of the wrong files; no backups had ever been made of the lost data base.

- a major research and development facility depending on temporary staffing for their data center operation experienced a two-day disruption when a disgruntled former employee returned unnoticed through the temporary employment agency and sabotaged the data center.

- a medium-size service organization experienced severe embarrassment and inconvenience as well as a five-figure dollar loss when their voicemail system crashed and all current messages were irretrievably lost.

- a large insurance company experienced a six-figure dollar loss when a utility power disruption forced their data center to rely on backup power. Although their uninterruptible power supply and backup generators were effective for the data center, several hundred employees were put out of work since there was no backup power for business operations in the same building.

- a bank was put out of business for over a week and very nearly permanently when a facility disruption necessitated activation of their data center disaster recovery program. Although the data center was operational in less than 48 hours at a recovery site, no business resumption plan had been implemented for the 100+ employees displaced by the same event.

- a hundred-employee service organization was nearly put out of business when flooding of the area around their offices prevented access to their building. Although they had an off-site recovery plan, their only file backups were stored in the computer room.

"Real disasters" are seldom obvious or direct; the World Trade Center attacks, the Loma Prieta Earthquake, the Hinsdale Central Office Fire, as profound as these events may have been, are but a small percentage of the 'disasters' facing the typical organization. The "typical" disaster is far more likely to look like the scenarios above. As often as not, they are compound failures gradually escalating from seemingly innocuous, recoverable glitches to near-tragedies. In most cases, human error (whether proactive or reactive, commission or omission) is the single greatest factor in growing a large headache into a small disaster.

How does one transform those large headaches into valuable learning experiences rather than into disasters?

- Aggressively look for and address weaknesses in your contingency plans. Use regular structured walkthroughs or even brainstorming sessions to isolate and resolve vulnerabilities.

- Frequently test your contingency plans to failure: find the weakest links, rather than striving to demonstrate a successful recovery test.

- Don't assume that 'real' disasters will look like the scenarios you have tested: your contingency plan should address every conceivable disaster scenario, yet assume that the 'real' disaster, which will be the ultimate test of the contingency plan, will be the one scenario which was not specifically considered.

---

*This article originally appeared in **InfoSecurity News** Magazine.*

REFERENCES

Availability.com — "IT Availability Checklist"
http://www.availability.com/elements/information_technology/index.cfm?fuseaction=checklist

"Business Continuity Glossary," DRJ/DRI, 2003, http://www.drj.com

FFIEC IT Examination Handbook, Business Continuity Planning Booklet, March 2003

Contingency Planning and Management Online. Volume VI, Number 5, September/October 2001.
http://www.contingencyplanning.com

Federal Emergency Management Agency, Emergency Management Guide for Business and Industry,
Sponsored by a Public-Private Partnership with the Federal Emergency Management Agency, June
2002.

Gartner Group, High Availability: A Perspective, September 20, 2001

National Institute of Technology and Standards, Special Publication, 800-26, Security Self
Assessment Guide for Information Technology Systems, August 2001.

National Institute of Technology and Standards, Special Publication 800-12, An Introduction to
Computer Security: The NIST Handbook, October 1995.

University of Texas Medical Branch., Payroll Business Continuity and Recovery Plan, February,
2003.

Seagate Technology, "Types of Backups," Technical Bulletin #4062.
http://www.certance.com/support/tape/index.html

References

(Continued)

National Institute of Standards and Technology, Special Publication 800-30, First Public Exposure DRAFT, Risk Management Guide, June 2001.

Pelant, Barney, E., "Business Impact Analysis," Professional Development Program, DRI, 2001

Purcell, F. J. Bud, "Who Does What (In the Event of a Disaster)," Disaster Recovery Journal, Vol. 8, 1995.

Rothstein, Philip J and Bailey, Thomas D, "Where Does it Hurt?" Contingency Journal, July - Sept. 1990.

Straits, George and Snow, Norman, "Business Continuity Planning: A Case History," Disaster Recovery Journal, Vol. 8, 1995.

Texas Department of Information Resources, Business Continuity Planning Guidelines, 1999

Wold, Geoffrey H., and Robert F. Shriver 1988, "Disaster Recovery For Banks"

Wold, Geoffrey, "The Disaster Recovery Process," Part II and III, Disaster Recovery Journal, Vol. 5, 1995.

SELECTED BUSINESS CONTINUITY BOOKS AND RESOURCES AVAILABLE FROM ROTHSTEIN ASSOCIATES INC.

www.rothstein.com

BUSINESS CONTINUITY: BEST PRACTICES — WORLD-CLASS BUSINESS CONTINUITY MANAGEMENT (2nd Edition) by Andrew Hiles, FBCI

"BUSINESS CONTINUITY: BEST PRACTICES provides a practical implementation framework for the ten core units of competence jointly established by the Disaster Recovery Institute International (DRII) and Business continuity Institute (BCI). It can be used as a step-by-step guide by those new to BC management or referred to by more seasoned professionals for ideas and updates on specific topics. The guide covers all units of competence decided upon by DRII and BCI, and adds further background based on the experience of the author. Examples are provided throughout the book -- all having their roots in real cases." — Information Security Magazine.

BCM FRAMEWORK™ CD-ROM by Andrew Hiles

BCM Framework™ consists of a number of easily tailored modules that are selected from a database of client work from a combined total of over one hundred years of consultancy experience — modules that are hand-picked as the most relevant to your own situation, culture, organization, equipment platform and infrastructure. It contains documents, examples, checklists and templates covering each of the DRII / BCI's ten disciplines, model project plans, questionnaires and Business Recovery Action Plans for with Organization Schematics and role descriptions, with some vital - and often forgotten - actions included. These are in MS Word®, MS Excel® and MS Project® formats designed to be easily tailored to your organization's needs.

EMOTIONAL TERRORS IN THE WORKPLACE: PROTECTING YOUR BUSINESS' BOTTOM LINE — EMOTIONAL CONTINUITY MANAGEMENT IN THE WORKPLACE
By Vali Hawkins Mitchell, Ph.D., LMHC; Philip Jan Rothstein, FBCI, Editor

"This book's goal is to arm the individual with enough information and structure to persuade the boss to take a shot at adding this skill and knowledge that will help managers and leaders preempt or at least begin to recognize the signs of corrosive emotional distress. This book is an eye-opener. There are many case histories with frequent efforts to connect the type of manager and management behavior to forecast success or the need for more effort. There is an interesting methodology for calculating the cost of emotional distress and disturbance. There are lists and descriptions of all types of employees and managers, and how to recognize the destructive emotional dislocations that category can cause. This book and your guidance can help your boss prepare for changes in their personal behavior and concept of management, fill a serious gap in their experience and training, and truly become an 'empathetic manager.'" — James E. Lukaszewski, ABC, APR, Fellow PRSA, Chairman, The Lukaszewski Group

More Selected Business Continuity Books and Resources
Available From Rothstein Associates Inc. — www.rothstein.com

ENTERPRISE RISK ASSESSMENT AND BUSINESS IMPACT ANALYSIS:
BEST PRACTICES by Andrew Hiles

This book demystifies risk assessment. In a practical and pragmatic way, it covers many techniques and methods of risk and impact assessment with detailed, practical examples and checklists. It explains, in plain language, risk assessment methodologies used by a wide variety of industries and provides a comprehensive toolkit for risk assessment and business impact analysis.

BUSINESS CONTINUITY PLANNING AND HIPAA: BUSINESS CONTINUITY MANAGEMENT IN THE HEALTH CARE ENVIRONMENT, by James C. Barnes
Deborah Barnes (Editor), Philip Jan Rothstein (Editor)

This book examines business continuity planning as adapted to encompass the requirements of The Health Care Portability and Accountability Act of 1996, or HIPAA. We examine the typical business continuity planning model and highlight how the special requirements of HIPAA have shifted the emphasis. The layout of this book was designed to afford assistance, hints, and templates to the person charged with the task of implementing business continuity planning into a healthcare organization.

DISASTER RECOVERY TESTING: EXERCISING YOUR CONTINGENCY PLAN
Philip Jan Rothstein, Editor

From this book, the contingency planner can understand more than just how to test: why to test, when to test (and not test) and the necessary participants and resources. Further, this book addresses some often-ignored, real-world considerations: the justification, politics and budgeting affecting recovery testing. By having multiple authors share their respective areas of expertise, it is hoped that this book will provide the reader with a comprehensive resource addressing the significant aspects of recovery testing.

BUSINESS CONTINUITY PROGRAM SELF-ASSESSMENT CHECKLIST WITH CD-ROM, by Edmond D. Jones

This book and companion CD-ROM contains a comprehensive set of questions to assess the status of an organization's business continuity program. The questions may be used by a new or experienced business continuity planner to assess the overall program to determine those areas needing work. The same checklists can be used by internal or external audit or by others having a responsibility for evaluating an organization's business continuity program.

BUSINESS THREAT AND RISK ASSESSMENT CHECKLIST
(WITH CD-ROM) by Edmond D. Jones

This manual contains checklists that an individual or group may use to evaluate the threats and risks which may impact an organization's campus, facility or even specific departments within the organization. Each of the checklists shown in this manual and a cover page that may be used to assemble your own checklists are contained on the CD that accompanies this manual.

AUDITING BUSINESS CONTINUITY: GLOBAL BEST PRACTICES
by Rolf von Roessing

"The work not only provides a general outline of how to conduct different types of audits but also reinforces their application by providing practical examples and advice to illustrate the step-by-step methodology, including contracts, reports and techniques. The practical application of the methodology enables the professional auditor and BCM practitioner to identify and illustrate the use of good BCM practice whilst demonstrating added value and business resilience." — Dr. David J. Smith, MBA LL.B(Hons), Chairman of the Business Continuity Institute, Education Committee

ABOUT THE AUTHOR

Kenneth L. Fulmer, CBCP, has been involved in the Business Continuity Planning field for over 14 years. He has been a member of the Disaster Recovery Institute International (DRII, www.drii.org) since 1991 and a Certified Business Continuity Planner since 1992. Mr. Fulmer's career has spanned 27 years in the computer-related industry and has published, trained and spoken on business continuity issues.

Ken began his career as a public school teacher in Silver Spring, MD, and has since been a Bank Officer for Imperial Bancorp; now Comerica Bancorp, New York, and a National Account Executive with Digital Equipment Corporation; now Hewlett Packard.

Ken's Third Edition of **Business Continuity Planning: A Step-by-Step Guide with Planning Forms on CD-ROM** builds upon the foundation of the two previous, highly successful editions.

How to Get Your FREE DOWNLOAD of Bonus Resource Materials for This Book

You're entitled to a free download of the *Toolkit* that accompanies your purchase of *Business Continuity Planning: A Step-by-Step Guide with Planning Forms, 3rd edition* by Ken Fulmer.

The Toolkit Download provides numerous sample plans, templates, and reproducible worksheets and forms, including a business vulnerability worksheet; Business Impact Assessment (BIA) sample questionnaire for departments; cumulative outage costs worksheet; emergency response team assignments and call sheet; vendor call sheet; sample test plan and maintenance plan, etc. There are also checklists/ corrective action forms for various natural hazards, including, fires, floods, winter storms, hurricanes, earthquakes and tornadoes, along with an emergency response plan (ERP) checklist. Checklists for special hazards include those for power outages, boiler failures, bomb threats, hazardous material spills, and civil unrest, along with a checklist for vital records storage. Additional resources include information about federal and state agencies, such as FEMA; bibliographies; articles and papers; and links to a variety of related websites.

To access these bonus materials, you only need to login to our website as an existing user or register as a new user, and then register your book by following the instructions.

IT'S EASY—LOGIN OR REGISTER YOURSELF ON OUR WEBSITE

1. FIRST, login as an existing user or register as a new user of our website at www.rothstein.com/register   New users will receive an email link to confirm.

THEN REGISTER YOUR BOOK

2. Logging in or registering takes you to our Product Registration page. You'll see a list of books. Select your book by clicking the corresponding link to the left and just follow the instructions.

3. Receive a confirming email with additional information and instructions.

IF YOU HAVE ANY QUESTIONS OR CONCERNS, PLEASE CALL OR EMAIL US:

Rothstein Associates Inc.
203.740.7444 or 1-888-ROTHSTE in   fax 203.740.7401
4 Arapaho Rd.   Brookfield, Connecticut   06804-3104 USA
Email: info@rothstein.com

CPSIA information can be obtained
at www.ICGtesting.com
Printed in the USA
BVOW10s1759160816

459172BV00004B/44/P